YES, YOU CAN...

Achieve Financial Independence

Yes, You Can...

Achieve Financial Independence

Includes the Stowers Financial Analysis CD-Rom

BY JAMES E. STOWERS
with Jack Jonathan

To Suzie
James E Stowers
4-15-2002

STOWERS
INNOVATIONS
INC
An American Century Company

Yes, You Can...Achieve Financial Independence
with Stowers Financial Analysis CD-Rom.
Third Edition
© 2000 by Stowers Innovations, Inc.

ISBN 0-9629788-2-5: $34.00
Library of Congress Card Number: 00-191348

*This book is dedicated to all of you who
are determined to become financially independent.*

*The material in this book is based on my personal
beliefs and opinions.*

*The information is presented for educational
purposes only and is not intended to recommend any
particular investment product or service.*

*Real life examples included in this book are pro-
vided simply for illustrative purposes to demonstrate
the principles discussed. In addition, various assumed
examples are given throughout the book. None of the
examples, real or assumed are intended to represent or
promote the performance history of a specific fund or
investment product.*

*Yes, You Can . . . Achieve Financial Independence
will last a lifetime.*

—James E. Stowers

Much of the credit for refining the content of this book goes to a team of editors who provided objective criticisms: Anne Davis, Mort Singer and Nancy Buckwalter began the process. Alan Doan, Amy Smith, Eric Flamholtz, Gordon Snyder, Gunnar Hughes, John Small, Myriam McCartney, Sheldon Stahl and Steve Winn added to the improvements with further insights. We also owe our thanks to our many friends and colleagues who read the various typescripts and offered excellent suggestions. We always found that each new review brought further improvement.

We are indebted to Todd Garren for his dedication and accuracy in compiling the extensive statistical data that appears throughout.

Our grateful thanks go to Paul Coker Jr., whose imaginative illustrations have enhanced the book. Moreover, Paul's insights improved the content with his knowledge of form matching his artistry.

Book designer Rick Cusick, along with the creative staff of Kansas City's Kuhn & Wittenborn Advertising, integrated the text, charts and illustrations into a harmonious whole.

We owe special recognition to Nancy O'Neill, Karen Hofferber and Sam Goller for the creative and production efforts in making this third edition possible.

Finally, the lion's share of credit must go to Virginia Stowers, Jim's beloved wife, who was always patient and supportive through countless events along the way.

> *I am determined to try to do my best*
> *at whatever I choose to do.*
>
> JAMES E. STOWERS

Part 1: About Money

We all use money, but few of us
understand its true nature.

- How Money Developed
- Precious Metals
- Paper Currency
- Banking and State Bank Notes
- The Birth of Today's Money System
- The Federal Reserve System
- Money in the 20th Century
- Money in Circulation

Money is not actually spent;
it is traded for something you want.

- How Can You Obtain Money?
- What Can You Do With Money?

An unwavering determination that nothing
was going to prevent me from accomplishing my goals...

*I am determined to try to do my best
at whatever I choose to do.*

James E. Stowers

I wrote this book because I wanted to share with you the beliefs and personal experiences that have contributed to my success. **Yes, You Can… Achieve Financial Independence** presents a different perspective on money. This book was written for people who would like to be financially independent – those who want to enjoy peace of mind in the future while being able to do what they want to do when they want to do it. One major concern today affecting people about to retire or who are retired is that they might outlive the sources of their income. Anyone, young or old, can benefit from my ideas.

Is it an accident that I became financially independent? No. My success did not come from luck, nor did it come from a family inheritance. Instead, it came as a result of:

My desire not to be controlled by circumstances;

An unwavering determination that **nothing** was going to prevent me from accomplishing my goals;

The determination to increase my knowledge through study and experience;

     and

Continuous effort.

When I was young, my father did not want me to work for money; he wanted me to concentrate on my studies and music. He also urged me to play. My first experience with money as a child in grade school was putting some of my allowance in a local bank savings account. I can vividly remember my surprise, several years later, when my mother took me to the bank to close out my account. The amount I received was only slightly more than I had put in! I learned that a savings account was a

I learned that a savings account was a money saver, not a money maker.

money saver, not a money maker.

I began to learn about investing when I graduated from college. I was fascinated with the opportunities it could give me to help people improve their financial positions – **and more importantly, their lives**.

In 1952, I began working for a national company representing a large mutual fund. In my desire to try to be the best, I felt I had to strive to know more than others. Fortunately, I found a mentor in George H. Wood, an officer of the management company. George helped me learn the business. When I reflect on my four decades of business experience, it's clear that few people have had more influence than George had on my life and on the way I think. Early in our relationship, George told me that he felt there were two ways to learn: study a few books by experts, or read the opinions of many people. When I assured him that I would like to know what a lot of people thought about a topic, he said he would suggest books for me to read – only if I agreed to study each one he selected.

He was a speed reader who reviewed hundreds of books, sharing with me only those he thought I should read. My experience with George was worth more than my two college degrees. In fact, I like to think that I've earned a third degree from the School of Hard Knocks.

At the time I was poring over George's selections, I was making my living entirely from commissions on the investments and life insurance policies I sold – I received no salary. When your livelihood depends entirely on sales commissions, you often learn the hard way, that how you **communicate** with people means everything – a fact George hammered home. "You're not there to tell people what they **should** do," George said. "Your job is to make them aware of what they **can** do." After meeting with a prospective client, I would sit down and reconstruct our conversation in writing, to make sure I had followed George's advice.

In this book, I will share with you many of the beliefs that ultimately formed the foundation for my success in business.

As I tried to help people improve their financial positions, it became apparent that they had to protect their families with life insurance before they could even think about starting an investment program. If I had encouraged them to do otherwise, it would have been a disservice.

During that time, few life insurance companies were willing to offer the kind of policy that would give people the most protection for the least amount of money. I became convinced that low-cost, permanent annual renewable term policies represented the best value. A group of

...he said he'd suggest books for me to read – only if I agreed to study each one he selected.

us who shared this belief decided to form a life insurance company that would offer a policy we were willing to buy ourselves. We wanted to give it a name that would best describe the type of insurance we planned to offer and came up with "Death Benefit Insurance Company." It was perhaps too accurate. Our medical director suggested we put a little life into it with the name "Survivors' Benefit Insurance Company." Of course, we agreed.

The company I was working for heard of our plans and told me to either forget them or leave, so I said good-bye.

We were proud of our life insurance company. As far as we know, it was the first company to offer **pure permanent annual renewable term insurance**, renewable to age 100.

While we were starting Survivors' Benefit, I also formed a broker-dealer firm to offer nationally known mutual funds. Our sales representatives were paid high commissions for selling these funds. By the end of our first year, the representatives were earning money, but our profits were not worth our efforts. I realized, if we were to become profitable as a company, I would have to start my own mutual fund. So, in 1958, I founded Twentieth Century Investors, Inc., now called American Century Mutual Funds, offering two mutual funds with initial assets of only $107,000. At first, we employed only four people. Later, in 1980, we chose to sell the life insurance company so that we could devote all of our efforts to the success of the mutual funds.

The mutual fund business grew slowly; but, by the year 2000, over 3,000 people managed and serviced over $100 billion in 70 different funds. Over time, we have won the confidence of more than 2,000,000 investors in our ability to manage money.

The financial figures in this edition were purposely not updated. Recent investment results could easily be viewed as unbelievable. Also, they might focus your attention away from the long-term, to short-term results. Updating the figures would detract from the principles that we are trying to convey.

Having finally succeeded after all these years, I have never lost my desire to try to be the best. I have always wanted to do my utmost to help people improve their financial positions so they can eventually become financially independent. I am still convinced that **if I help people become successful, they, in turn, will help me become successful**.

As one result of my success, my wife, Virginia, and I have been able to create the Stowers Institute of Medical Research. We want to give back something *more valuable than money* to the millions of people who made our success possible. Through this Institute, we are dedicated to making a significant contribution in medical research by expanding the understanding of the secrets of life. We are committed to improving the quality of life by paving the way for new approaches to the causes, treatment, and prevention of diseases such as cancer.

If you are determined to improve your financial position and to strive for financial independence, you need to be aware of the opportunities that are available and of the many principles and facts that can affect your future. To start with, you need to have a prepared mind. It is helpful to better understand money – its history, uses and potential. In addition, it is important to fully comprehend the extraordinary power of compounding, the shrinking value of a dollar and the crucial importance of time in investing.

This book will lead you through the "financial forest" as painlessly as possible, with touches of humor, a sprinkling of philosophy and a heavy dose of hard facts. **READ IT, DIGEST IT, APPLY IT. This process may be one of the most important financial undertakings of your life.**

About Money

A Brief History of Money

A Brief History of Money

*We all use money, but few
of us understand its true nature.*

How Money Developed

Long ago no one needed money. Our ancestors grew their own food or hunted for it. As their skills evolved, many people realized they were better at performing some tasks, while others found satisfaction in accomplishing other chores.

In time, man's desire to acquire something he could not make or grow inspired him to start trading his particular skills or goods for services or products someone else could provide. Trading articles or services without the use of money is called "bartering." Anthropologists believe that tribes in Europe and Asia routinely met to exchange goods as early as 12,000 years ago.

Bartering worked fairly well for thousands of years but it was cumbersome and often inconvenient. A farmer wanting to trade corn for a mule had to find a mule owner who wanted corn. If the mule owner wanted an axe rather than corn, the farmer was out of luck. He could search for an axe maker who would take corn and then trade for the mule, but that took time.

Tomatoes might be valuable...but only if they were not held too long.

Value was also a problem – it constantly changed. One day an axe might be exchanged for a mule or a small cow, but not for a bushel of corn. Two weeks later, a hungry tool maker might willingly trade axes for corn. It was difficult to agree on a standard of value for making trades, and **it was not easy to save or store up the things determined valuable.** Tomatoes might be valuable – but only if they were not held too long.

Bars of crystal salt were used as money in many parts of Africa. Offering a bar of salt to be licked became a courtesy when one met a friend. This social custom was considered a luxury that only a few privileged people could afford.

In North America, Indians traded with "wampum" – beads made from the inner whorls of sea shells that were polished and strung together in belts. The beads were two colors, black and white; black beads were twice as valuable as white. Early settlers of New England used wampum as money when trading with the Indians for furs. In the 1700s, grain, fish, gunpowder and shot were popular forms of money.

Interestingly, beer was once a form of currency. It was used as a partial payment of wages in English coal mines during the 1850s. A commission was sent to investigate beer's efficiency as money. It reported that **this "money" was popular, highly liquid, but was issued to excess, and was difficult to store.**

In all these cases, items were accepted in trade only if they were considered to have real value. But many goods had built-in drawbacks that limited their usefulness as money.

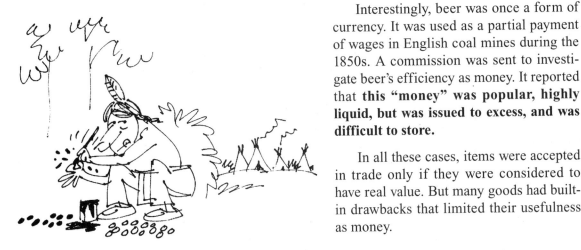

Black beads were
twice as valuable
as white.

Ideally, money should be:

- Easy to handle

- Reliable, so that it may serve as a predictable and constant standard of value over time

- Universally accepted as a medium of exchange

- Divisible into easily identifiable units of measurement

Precious Metals

Historians do not agree on where, when, or how precious metals were first used as money. Widely separate societies were attracted at different times by the glitter and sparkle of silver and gold. Because gold and silver were both hard to find and in great demand, someone offering precious metals could command more goods.

The Chinese used gold cubes as early as 2100 B.C., and the Bible mentions precious metals. The earliest known coins, cast in Greece around 700 B.C., were crudely inscribed gold and silver ovals. But gold and silver coins were not immune to periodic problems. For instance, Alexander the Great brought so much precious metal home from his conquests that the value of gold and silver in Greece dropped by one-third.

Paper Currency

A new form of money emerged in the Middle Ages in Europe. Because large quantities of coins were cumbersome and unsafe to transport, people taking long trips would leave their coins with goldsmiths for safekeeping and take, in return, the goldsmiths' receipt, which was worthless to a robber. At the traveler's destination, the receipt was exchanged for coins by an associate of the goldsmith. The receipts became so commonplace that people began paying debts with them rather than with coins. This marked the beginning of paper money.

The receipts became so commonplace that people began paying debts with them rather than with coins. This marked the beginning of paper money.

The use of paper money increased greatly after 1650 with the rise of national banks. For example, the Bank of Sweden, founded in 1656, printed paper bank notes which were issued to people who deposited money. These notes stated the amount of coins that a person would receive from the bank.

Years later in America, the Congress of the original 13 colonies had to finance an army during the Revolutionary War. With no taxing powers, the Congress turned to the printing presses. People were bitterly opposed to the increased amount of paper money because it lowered money's value and created higher prices for goods and services.

Banking and State Bank Notes

The United States Treasury, formed in 1789, lacked enough precious metal to issue all the coins the growing economy needed. Thus, at the local level, banks took deposits in gold and silver and made loans and payments in notes they created, which were redeemable in gold and silver. State bank notes were used widely during much of the 1800s, and by the early 1860s, more than 10,000 separate note issues of different sizes, colors and designs were in circulation. Banks had to keep a precious metal reserve on hand to meet requests for withdrawals.

...by the early 1860s more than 10,000 separate note issues of different sizes, colors and designs were in circulation.

State bank notes worked well only where people felt confident that their bank was sound and that notes could be redeemed at any time. If depositors feared a bank would not redeem their notes, they would rush to cash in their deposits for gold or silver before the reserves disappeared.

In the early 1800s, America had many honest, well-managed banks, but some earned a reputation for fraud. Even before state laws regulated banks to assure the public that the reserves were safe, vaults were built so that customers could view the precious metals. Less honest bankers piled gold or silver coins on top of kegs of nails. When state examiners were sent to check reserves, some slick bank officers shipped money from bank to bank, only minutes ahead of the examiner!

The Birth of Today's Money System

The American Civil War produced changes that set the stage for today's money system. At that time, the federal government was unable to raise enough money through taxes to pay for the conflict. As rapidly as the Treasury paid bills with gold and silver coin, the metal was hoarded.

Reluctantly, Congress issued United States notes that were not redeemable in gold or silver. Congress tried to make the notes acceptable by declaring them **legal tender,** which meant that they had to be accepted in payment of all private debts.

The federal government also began chartering national banks that were given paper currency to issue. National banks received currency in proportion to the amount of government bonds they purchased. However, as the government paid off its debts after the war, the number of bonds used as backing for currency shrank. As a result, the amount of money in circulation declined, and the cash supply became inadequate to meet the needs of industry and trade. This condition led to periodic money panics until 1913 when the banking system was restructured.

The Federal Reserve System

In the early 20th century, most banks kept little cash. Small country banks deposited cash reserves at larger banks, which in turn deposited the reserves at big-city banks. This money was available to lend to businesses and brokers. This accumulation of reserves in the big-city banks hurt banks as well as the public. For instance, a bumper crop of grain would create a sudden demand for cash and cause country banks to ask for the reserves to be returned. In providing these reserves, big-city banks were left with little cash to meet the demands of their customers. Eventually, their cash ran so low that a panic started.

A severe panic in 1907 sparked the reform movement that caused Congress to create the Federal Reserve System in 1913. This system of twelve regional reserve banks was established to manage the reserves of all nationally chartered banks. The Federal Reserve Board of Governors in Washington, D.C., supervised and administered the overall operations of the system — and still does today.

The Federal Reserve banks lent funds to member banks so they could meet sudden and unexpected withdrawals...

The Federal Reserve lent funds to member banks so they could meet sudden and unexpected withdrawals, thus avoiding cash shortages that triggered earlier panics. Each Federal Reserve bank issued its own notes, known today as Federal Reserve Notes. These gold-backed notes were issued when each region's currency needs arose. When demand for currency decreased, the notes were returned to the Federal Reserve banks as reserves for commercial banks. Thus, money was available as needed.

Money in the 20th Century

When the value of coin and paper money was tied to gold, industrial nations often had "boom" or "bust" economies. Rising gold holdings, either from new discoveries or international trade payments, increased the nation's money in circulation. If the amount of money rose faster than production output, prices soared. If gold holdings didn't keep pace with production output, prices fell and workers were laid off.

Today most money is "fiat" money; money created almost as if by magic. It is without gold backing but must be accepted as legal tender by virtue of the government's declaration.

While the use of paper money without the backing of gold and silver had been tried during the Civil War (1861-65), the modern era of **fiat money** began during the Depression in the 1930s, when most nations abandoned the rigid use of gold money and gold-backed currency. Today, most coin and currency is "fiat" money, created almost as if by magic. It is without gold backing but must be accepted as legal tender by virtue of the government's declaration. This money relies solely on the public's trust in the government. Fiat money isn't valuable in itself and does not represent a claim on gold or silver. **Money's value lies in its purchasing power.**

The story of money has been punctuated with episodes when the value of money declined dramatically. After World War I, Germany saw the worst inflation of any modern industrial country. The value of its paper money fell so low that currency was a cheaper fuel than firewood. Although economists have known for centuries that changes in the amount of money in circulation and the speed at which it is spent affect business, they didn't discover how the relationship worked until this century.

Money in Circulation

Most countries have central banks that attempt to balance the money available for spending by controlling bank reserves and bank lending – the activity that creates new money. In the United States, the Federal Reserve System is responsible for making sure that banks don't create so much money that we have inflation, or so little money that we have a recession.

The job isn't easy. No central bank has been entirely successful in maintaining the balance between too much and too little money. One problem the Federal Reserve faces is how to balance the supply of money with other major factors that affect the economy and inflation, such as government spending and taxing. Another problem is that people are unable to agree on just how much money is enough.

No central bank has been entirely successful in maintaining the balance between too much and too little money.

Just as we have gone from cows to wampum to gold, in the future the form of money transactions may change dramatically – for instance, it may take the form of "smart cards" containing a computer chip which stores the remaining dollar balance of the card after a purchase is made. The Internet has also opened up countless possibilities to reduce more traditional forms of money transactions.

One problem the Federal Reserve faces is how to balance the supply of money with … government spending and taxing.

Money is worth
only what you can
exchange for it.

Sources and Uses of Money

Money is not actually spent;
   it is traded for something you want.

Money is the universal medium of exchange for goods and services. It allows us to trade **value for value,** a means of trade without exchanging precious metals or bartering.

Money is worth only what you can exchange for it. In most instances, it is unlikely that you are going to exchange your money for services or goods unless you believe that the value of what you want is equal to or greater than the value you place on your cash.

How Can You Obtain Money?

Money is usually earned through wages, salaries, bonuses and commissions as a result of your effort, hard work and creativity. There is only a certain amount of money you can bring home from your personal efforts, and there is only a limited time for you to do so. Money can also come from your investments – that is, dividends, capital gains and interest. At retirement, money can come from earnings on savings, from a retirement plan and from Social Security. Money sometimes comes from gifts and inheritance or, if you are extremely lucky, from a lottery or a roll of the dice.

How can you obtain money?

What Can You Do With Money?

Money is not actually spent; it is traded for something you want. "Spending" money does not accurately describe the financial transaction. Spending implies that the dollars in the transaction disappeared, that they were used up or consumed in some way. "Trading" money more accurately describes what happens in a transaction. **Money is not consumed; it remains in circulation.**

Money is not actually spent; it is traded for something you want.

You can do many things with money. Such as:

- **Trading**

- **Lending**

- **Borrowing**

- **Keeping**

- **Giving it away**

Trading Money

Through money, you can trade the value of your services for something you want or need. If someone wants you to perform a service, you'll receive money in exchange. In this case, you are trading your time and effort for money. Later, you can trade the money you earned for goods and services you want.

The moment you trade your dollars, you no longer have them. You have something else.

The moment you trade your dollars, you no longer have them. You have something else. If you trade all of your available dollars for any one thing, you do not have that money to trade for anything else. Also, you can trade a certain sum only once. You can't trade the same money again.

Dollars can be traded for items that are consumed, such as food and clothing, or for services, such as legal assistance, health care and utilities. Money can be traded for investment ownership in items such as a home, a mutual fund or common stock. You can trade for collectibles, such as stamps, coins, art, antiques and jewelry.

✦ Lending Money

You can lend your money to individuals or institutions with the understanding that you will be paid a fixed sum of money (interest) for its use over an agreed amount of time. Then, at the end of that period, the full amount you lent will be returned to you.

Some examples of loans are:

> Savings account at a bank, savings and loan or credit union
>
> Certificates of Deposit
>
> Personal loans
>
> Government, corporate or municipal bonds

In certain transactions, you may believe you are buying something when in fact you are lending your money. For example, when you buy a Certificate of Deposit, you are making a loan to a bank.

✦ Borrowing Money

When you borrow, you pay a fixed sum (interest) regularly for use of the money over an agreed amount of time. At the end of that period, you agree to pay back the amount you originally borrowed. When you borrow money you are committing some of your future income. You are spending money you have not yet earned which has to be repaid from future earnings. If you spend the money on luxuries, you may temporarily improve your style of living, but not your financial position. On the other hand, if you borrow money to invest, i.e., "leveraging," you could improve your future financial position. Leveraging is using borrowed money to own an investment that is expected to provide higher earnings and profits than the cost of borrowing.

When you borrow money you are committing some of your future income.

Normally, the higher the risk to the lender, the higher the interest rate you are required to pay. When borrowing for an investment, the rate is often lower if the investment is used and accepted by the lender as collateral.

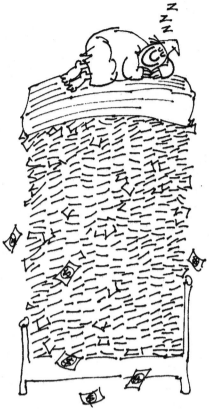

In the old days,
people saved
money under
their mattresses . . .

◆ Keeping Money

*If money is kept in a
safe deposit box,
potential income
and profits
are lost.*

Instead of trading your money, you can keep it so that it is available to trade later for something you may want. In the old days, people saved money under their mattresses or in a cookie jar. Today you can use a safe deposit box. But, if money is kept there, potential income and profits are lost.

◆ Giving Money Away

There are many reasons for a gift of money. The act of giving generates a shared thought from the giver to the receiver. Giving money away takes many forms, such as wills, trusts or simple donations.

. . . or in a cookie jar.

The Shrinking Dollar

The Shrinking Dollar

The dollar bill has shrunk in size –
but not nearly as much as it has shrunk in value.

Compare the relative size of the 1917 bill with the size of today's $1 bill. Today's dollar is quite a bit smaller than the older one.

(3-1)

The dollar bill has shrunk in size, but not nearly as much as it has shrunk in value.

(Illustrations of dollar bills shown at 60% of original size.)

If the **value** of today's dollar were compared with a 1900 dollar bill, you would find that it had shrunk by more than 95%. In other words, what you could buy a century ago for one dollar, would only get you a nickel's worth of goods today.

The risk of **losing money** is obvious. However, the danger of money **losing value** over time is not always recognized. Sadly for many, the process by which money loses value is often understood too late, if at all.

...money is worth only what it can be exchanged for at the time of a trade.

Remember, money is worth only what it can be exchanged for at the time of a trade. The dollar has lost value when it takes more dollars to trade for items now than it did before. When you go to the store and trade $1 for bread that you previously could have bought for 50 cents, you realize your dollar has lost one-half of its value.

The following chart illustrates the decline in the value of a dollar since 1900.

(3-2)   *Decline in Value of the Dollar Since 1900*

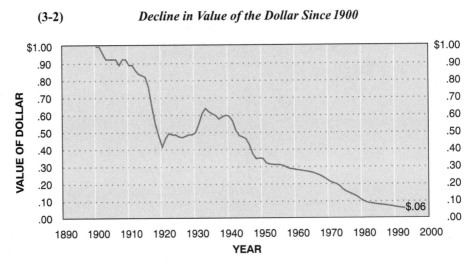

Source: Data provided by Bureau of the Census and Bureau of Labor Statistics.

As can be seen in the preceding chart, except for a few short periods, the dollar has lost value since 1900. While the dollar is still physically there, its exchange value has shrunk considerably. In fact, the value of a dollar has fallen since 1900 at an average rate of slightly more than 3% per year. During this time period, this rate has fluctuated. For example, throughout much of the 1960's, the rate of inflation averaged less than 3%. The 1970's, however, were marked by the dramatic increase in energy prices, as well as an acceleration in the inflation rate that lasted into the early 1980's. In the remainder of the 1980's, inflation slowed to an annual rate of 4%. And in the 1990's, further progress has been made in reducing the annual rate of inflation to 3% per year. Even if we concede to significant progress on the inflation front, the dollar continues to shrink in value.

Except for a few short periods, the dollar has continuously lost value since 1900.

Learning First-Hand About the Shrinking Dollar

While I was in the service during World War II, I bought United States Government Savings Bonds to help the war effort and to save money. These bonds were purchased for $18.75. The government agreed to buy them back for $25 at maturity. Years later, I tendered these savings bonds back to the government, which lived up to its agreement and paid me $25 for each bond.

The government received $18.75 from me, kept my money for over 10 years, and then paid me $25. By that time, each dollar was worth only about 50 cents. In addition, they collected tax from me on the $6.25 interest I had earned ($25.00 - $18.75 = $6.25 interest).

I gave an $18.75 value and, 10 years later, received a $12.50 value. I was patriotic, but I learned an important financial lesson from the experience.

I gave an $18.75 value and, 10 years later, received a $12.50 value. I was patriotic, but I learned an important financial lesson from the experience.

Picture yourself as a member of Congress in Washington, D.C.... Would you have the courage to suggest that everyone's taxes be raised?

Will a Dollar Continue to Lose Value?

No one knows if the value of a dollar will continue to decline. But what has happened to a dollar in the past gives us a good indication of what may happen in the future. Consider some facts:

- Our country carries an enormous debt, the product of many years of budget deficits.

- Although the federal budget has been balanced in recent years, the debt itself remains.

- Politicians are always tempted by new spending programs, which could create new deficits, forcing the government to issue new debt obligations.

The financial problems of the government keep mounting. Picture yourself as a member of Congress in Washington, D.C. Now assume that you and your colleagues are faced with the problem of finding billions to help a troubled industry. How would you go about finding that money? Would you have the courage to suggest that everyone's taxes be raised? What would the people you represent think? It is apparent many elected officials fear the wrath of public opinion more than a rising national debt.

The government's need for funds **is not limited** by the requirement that money must be convertible into gold on demand. If Congress votes to expand the debt limit as it has done on many occasions, and thereby allows the Treasury to issue additional financial obligations, **the new debt will most likely serve as the source of new money in the economy.** Would many people complain? Probably not, because over the years they have become accustomed to having an unbalanced budget. For these reasons and others, the rate of loss in the value of a dollar has the potential not just to continue, but to accelerate its decline.

If a dollar loses 6.7% of its value each year for 10 years, its value will be 50 cents.

If a dollar loses 6.7% of its value each year for 10 years, its value will be 50 cents. I fear this is very likely to happen in the future, although I hope otherwise. **If it does happen however, this loss in value is probably the biggest long-term financial risk you face.** If the dollar continues to lose value every year at that rate of 6.7%, it would be worth only 12.5 cents in 30 years.

In one respect, the trouble in the United States is that the rate of loss in the value of a dollar is not occurring quickly enough! People don't realize it's happening. If the dollar lost 15% or more of its value in one year, that would certainly capture everyone's attention. Things might change in Washington.

In one respect...
the rate of loss in the
value of the dollar is
not occurring quickly
enough.

Consequences of a Shrinking Dollar

If you should realistically assume a continued decrease in the value of a dollar, what does it mean? How might this affect you? To illustrate, assume that the value of a dollar were to decrease in the future at a rate of 50% every 10 years.

Everything you buy will cost twice as much. This means your income will have to double during those 10 years in order for you to maintain the same standard of living you have today. Any investments will have to double just to **stay even** – that is, multiply fourfold in 20 years, and eightfold in 30 years.

Consequences of a shrinking dollar.

For example, assume you traded $100,000 for a home today. From this time on, **your home will have its own intrinsic value. It will not be tied to the value of a dollar.** This intrinsic value will rise or fall based on the prevailing market for homes in your neighborhood but will not be affected by the value of a dollar. In 30 years, you can trade your home back into dollars **based on the value of a dollar at that time.** If the intrinsic value of your home remained the same as it was 30 years ago, and if a dollar's value declined 6.7% each year over that time, theoretically, your home could be sold (traded) for eight times as many dollars as you paid for it – in other words, $800,000. In this example, the important concept is that your home **did not** actually rise in value. Rather, a dollar lost so much value that someone else would have to trade eight times as many dollars to buy it.

If your home lost some intrinsic worth during this 30-year period, because of some factor such as neglect or a deteriorating neighborhood, you might have to take less than $800,000 for it. Likewise, if the intrinsic value of your home increased during those 30 years, you might be able to trade it for more than $800,000. As you can see, a combination of factors determines the final value. **Two different "values" are involved in this example: one, the real value of the home,**

and two, the value of a dollar at a given time.

What direct effect has the continuous loss in the value of a dollar had on people? In the "good old days," in 1834, you could have paid for a dinner for four in one of New York's prime restaurants, left a generous tip, and received change – all from a single dollar bill.

(3-3)

DELMONICO'S

RESTAURANT.
494 • PEARL • STREET.

BILL OF FARE

	Cents		Cents
Cup Tea or Coffee	1	Pork Chops	4
Bowl " "	2	Pork and Beans	4
Crullers	1	Sausages	4
Soup	2	Puddings.	4
Fried or Stewed Liver	3	Liver and Bacon	5
" " Heart	3	Roast Beef or Veal	5
Hash	3	Roast Mutton	5
Pies	4	Veal Cutlet.	5
Half Pie	2	Chicken Stew	5
Beef or Mutton Stew	4	Fried Eggs	5
Corn Beef and Cabbage	4	Ham and Eggs	10
Pigs Head " "	4	Hamburger Steak.	10
Fried Fish	4	Roast Chicken	10
Beef Steak	4		

Regular Dinner 12 Cents.

Do you think that the 1834 menu is too extreme an example? If so, ask your parents or people their age what it was like years ago. Ask them:

THEN	NOW
How much did they pay for their first home?	What do they think it would be worth today?
What did their first new car cost?	How much would a similar car cost now?
How much did four years of college cost?	What is the cost of a college education today?
How much did they pay for a loaf of bread?	How much does a loaf of bread cost today?

I can remember in the 1940s when 10 cents bought a loaf of bread. The other day I paid $1.85.

The cost of a loaf of bread, then and now, illustrates the loss in value of your money. How much does a loaf of bread cost today?

At this point, you can see how **people who kept their money in a "safe" place** (like the mattress or a cookie jar), thinking they were doing the right thing, **were losing real value year after year.**

One way to avoid the loss in the value of your money is to trade it quickly. Obviously, however, this move leaves you with no money in reserve for the future.

Another approach is to trade your money for something **not tied to a dollar,** something that has an opportunity to appreciate faster than the inevitable decline in the value of a dollar.

When dollars are accumulated or conserved for short periods (a few years) before being spent, the erosion in value of a dollar is limited. However, when dollars are accumulated or held for extended periods (10 to 20 years or more), such as for retirement, then the reality of money losing substantial value over time has potentially devastating consequences that must be taken into account in your financial planning.

If you truly want to be financially independent, it would be wise to plan for the event that a dollar would lose the highest percent of its value you believe it could possibly lose over time. This will give you the means to provide what you want, when you want it. If a dollar does not lose as much value as you thought, you would be much better off financially.

While I hope otherwise, I believe a dollar could lose 6.7% of its value each year. You will find this worse case assumption in various illustrations throughout the book.

If the Indians had invested those $24 they were paid for Manhattan Island at 7%, today they could buy it back and have money left over.

The Extraordinary Power of Compounding

*"Time is money," but money is not nearly
as valuable without time.*

The Dutch bought Manhattan Island from the Indians in 1626 – over 374 years ago – and they allegedly paid $24 for it. Were the Indians taken advantage of? If they had invested those $24 at 5% for 374 years, the investment would be worth $1.4 billion. That's assuming no taxes, of course.

(4-1)   ***$24 Invested for 374 Years (No Taxes)
at Various Rates of Return***

(Compounded Annually)

5%	$ 1,434,445,000
6%	46,501,160,000
7%	1,459,007,000,000
8%	44,333,243,000,000
9%	1,305,377,000,000,000
10%	37,267,194,000,000,000

Nature Is a Wonderful Teacher

Look at the amazing results of planting a single seed of wheat. One seed, when planted and nurtured, can produce more than 100 seeds. **If all of these seeds were not consumed but planted** with equal tender loving care, they would produce at least 10,000 more seeds of wheat. Nature is a wonderful teacher. She can help us understand what can happen when money is allowed to compound over time.

The Importance of Time and Money

Solomon said, **"In all of your getting, get understanding."** In few areas is there less understanding than in the subject of money. Most people find it difficult to comprehend precisely what money is. For

example, is $100,000 a large sum of money or a small amount? Before you jump to a conclusion, let's find out what this sum is really worth to you in your everyday life.

If you were paid your salary once in your lifetime, it might well amount to over $1,000,000. But that would be just a figure on paper until converted into a lifetime of rent or mortgage payments, groceries, clothing and utility bills.

You know better than anyone what your paycheck represents

Most people find it difficult to comprehend precisely what money is.

to you. When you think of your income in terms of how much it will buy each month, you begin to understand the real value of money. To understand how much $100,000 is really worth, consider that sum as a monthly dollar amount (ignoring taxes).

If you put $100,000 in a safe place and decided to TAKE OUT equal monthly amounts for 35 years, you would be able to TAKE OUT $238 each month. After 35 years, you would have nothing left. Now, if you **invested** your $100,000 and received a 6% rate of return, Table 4-2 shows that you would receive $487 income a month FOREVER on $100,000 without invading your principal. In summary, if you had invested your money for 35 years, you could have received a total of $204,540 ($487 x 12 months x 35 years = $204,540) and **still** have your original $100,000.

When you think of your income in terms of how much it will buy each month, you begin to understand the real value of money.

The monthly amount you received could have been increased by adding a portion of your principal to the earned income, thus using all

(4-2)

The Amount You Can Receive Monthly
From a $100,000 Investment

(Compounded Annually)

(%)	If You Receive Both Income and Part of the Principal				OR	If You Receive Income Only Keeping Principal FOREVER
0	$1,667	$556	$333	$238		$0
4	1,838	736	524	439		327
6	1,926	835	635	560		487
8	2,014	940	753	690		643
10	2,104	1,048	879	827		797
12	2,194	1,161	1,008	967		949
14	2,284	1,277	1,141	1,109		1,098
16	2,376	1,395	1,276	1,251		1,245
Years	5	15	25	35		

of your principal within a certain period of time. For example, if you had received a 6% rate of return on your money and you wanted nothing left after 35 years, the table above shows that you could have received $560 each month for that period. If, on the other hand, you wanted to use all of your money sooner, you could have received $835 a month for 15 years at a 6% rate of return.

If you were paid your salary once in your lifetime, it might well amount to over $1,000,000 …

(4-3)

How Much Cash Does It Take Monthly to Provide What You Want?

(Compounded Annually)

AGE AT START — PUT IN MONTHLY to age 65

(%)	20	30	40	50	60
0	$185.19	$238.10	$333.33	$555.56	$1,667
4	67.62	111.12	196.52	408.74	1,511
6	38.13	72.80	147.87	348.54	1,439
8	20.81	46.67	110.01	296.20	1,371
10	11.09	29.42	81.08	250.98	1,306
12	5.82	18.32	59.30	212.11	1,245
14	3.03	11.31	43.12	178.87	1,186
16	1.57	6.94	31.21	150.57	1,131
YEARS	45	35	25	15	5

AGE 65

AGE ENDING / **FOREVER** — TAKE OUT MONTHLY from age 65

	70	80	90	100	FOREVER	(%)
	$1,667	$556	$333	$238	$0	0
	1,838	736	524	439	327	4
	1,926	835	635	560	487	6
	2,014	940	753	690	643	8
	2,104	1,048	879	827	797	10
	2,194	1,161	1,008	967	949	12
	2,284	1,277	1,141	1,109	1,098	14
	2,376	1,395	1,276	1,251	1,245	16
YEARS	5	15	25	35		

How Much Cash Does It Take Monthly to Provide a Monthly Income Later?

Table 4-3 highlights one of the most important concepts in this entire book – **the extraordinary power of compounding over time.** The figures in the left square represent the amount of money necessary to PUT IN each month from a given age to age 65. The figures to the right are the monthly TAKE OUT figures beginning at age 65. The TAKE OUT figures are shown for various time periods and at various compound rates of return. They represent the amount of money that can be paid to you each month from both income and principal in order to deplete all of the money by the end of a stated number of years.

The boxed column at the extreme right represents the amount of money that you can TAKE OUT each month at various rates of return FOREVER and at the same time preserve the principal sum.

Let's consider some examples to better understand the message you can derive from it. The time you take reading and re-reading to understand the principles in this chapter can pay big dividends when you are older.

If you are 20 years old and your money can earn only a 6% rate of return, you can PUT IN $38.13 each month from age 20 to age 65 – for 45 years. Beginning at age 65, you can TAKE OUT $560 each month for the next 35 years or until you reach age 100. Over the 45 years, you would PUT IN a total of $20,590 and you can TAKE OUT $235,200 from age 65 to 100 at $560 a month.

If you are more interested in spending money than in saving it, and you delay investing until age 40 to accomplish the same goal, you would have to set aside an additional $109.74 a month for the next 25 years. You would have to PUT IN $147.87 each month – not $38.13 a month. During the 25 years up to age 65, you would PUT IN a total of $44,361 in order to receive the same $235,200 from age 65 to 100.

If you are more interested in spending money than in saving it, you may soon regret not paying closer attention to your financial future.

So you see, if you delayed 20 years, it would be necessary for you to PUT IN an additional $23,771 (or twice as much) in order to have the same amount you could have had by starting at age 20.

If you delayed investing until age 50 (30 years later), you would have to PUT IN $348.54 a month at 6% in order to TAKE OUT, at age 65, $560 a month until you reached 100. Over the 15-year period, you would PUT IN a total of $62,737 (over three times as much), and you would TAKE OUT $235,200 by the time you reached 100.

Remember: It is essential to start saving regularly early in life!

Time Is Truly Money

Time, as you can see from this review, is a vital factor in any serious discussion of money. The table below further underscores this point.

(4-4)   *TIME is a Vital Factor*
Using **6** percent compounded annually:

If you PUT IN	You could TAKE OUT
$ 1.00 a month for 45 years	*$14.69 a month for 35 years
$ 1.00 a month for 35 years	$ 7.69 a month for 35 years
$ 1.00 a month for 25 years	$ 3.79 a month for 35 years
$ 1.00 a month for 15 years	$ 1.61 a month for 35 years
$ 1.00 a month for 5 years	$ .39 a month for 35 years

*From Table 4-3, $560 ÷ $38.13 = $14.69

What Happens If You Can Earn Just 2% More?

Table 4-3 shows what could happen if your money earned 8% instead of 6%. If you PUT IN $20.81 a month from age 20 to age 65, you could TAKE OUT $690 a month to age 100. In this example, you would

PUT IN a total of $11,237 over the 45 years. By taking out $690 a month to age 100, you would TAKE OUT a total of $289,800. The difference between these two figures ($289,800 - $11,237 = $278,563) again illustrates the power of compounding over time.

There are two major benefits of reaching for an 8% rate of return instead of 6%. The first benefit is that you PUT IN $9,353 **less** over 45 years. The second benefit is that you TAKE OUT $54,600 **more** over 35 years. The total increased benefit of reaching **2% more** here would amount to $63,953...**the magic of compounding** at work.

	6%	vs.	8%	Advantage of greater return over time
PUT IN over 45 years	$ 20,590		$ 11,237	$ 9,353
TAKE OUT over 35 years	$235,200		$289,800	$54,600
Total Advantage				$63,953

Both the **importance of time and the advantage of an increased annual rate of return** are again stressed when you compare the table below to Table 4-4.

(4-5)   *The Importance of TIME*
Using **8** percent compounded annually:

If you PUT IN	You could TAKE OUT
$ 1.00 a month for 45 years	*$33.16 a month for 35 years
$ 1.00 a month for 35 years	$14.78 a month for 35 years
$ 1.00 a month for 25 years	$ 6.27 a month for 35 years
$ 1.00 a month for 15 years	$ 2.33 a month for 35 years
$ 1.00 a month for 5 years	$ .50 a month for 35 years

*From Table 4-3, $690 ÷ $20.81 = $33.16

... seeking higher returns generally increases the risk.

In summary, the two critical factors in the magic of compounding are (1) **the average annual rate of return** and (2) **time.** Of these two, the most fundamental is **time.** Deferring the decision to save is costly. Every year you delay saving, makes the goal of financial independence **much more difficult.**

The higher the rate of return you can achieve, the less money you must set aside each month to accomplish your goal. However, seeking higher returns generally increases the risk. If you started at age 30, Table 4-3 indicates that at 6%, you would need to set aside $72.80 each month to age 65 to receive $560 each month to age 100. Now, if you could instead earn a rate of 8% on your money (only 2% more), and you wanted to receive the same $560 each month to age 100, it is **not** necessary for you to set aside $46.67 a month as shown in Table 4-3, (which would enable you to receive $690 a month), but rather $37.88; i.e., ($46.67 ÷ $690) x $560 = $37.88. In other words, by reaching for 8%, the amount of money that you would need to **PUT IN** to accomplish your goal ($560) would be greatly reduced (from $72.80 to $37.88). Thus, a one-third increase in the rate of return reduced the required monthly amount by nearly one-half.

How Much CASH Does It Take NOW in One Lump Sum to Provide a Monthly Income LATER?

The higher the rate of return you can achieve, the less money you must set aside each month to accomplish your goal.

In comparison, instead of setting aside money each month, how much money would you have to set aside in a single lump sum earning 6% to accomplish the same goal of receiving $560 each month from age 65 to age 100? The shaded portion of Table 4-6 indicates the amount of money necessary at various ages to illustrate this point.

(4-6)

One Lump Sum
How Much Cash Does It Take Now to Provide What You Want?
(Compounded Annually)

(%)	AGE AT START							AGE 65	AGE ENDING				KEEPING PRINCIPAL FOREVER	(%)
	Birth	10	20	30	40	50	60		70	80	90	100		
0	$100,000.00	$100,000.00	$100,000	$100,000	$100,000	$100,000	$100,000		$1,667	$556	$333	$238	$0	0
4	7,813.27	11,565.55	17,120	25,342	37,512	55,526	82,193		1,838	736	524	439	327	4
6	2,265.26	4,056.74	7,265	13,011	23,300	41,727	74,726		1,926	835	635	560	487	6
8	672.13	1,451.09	3,133	6,763	14,602	31,524	68,058		2,014	940	753	690	643	8
10	203.93	528.94	1,372	3,588	9,230	23,939	62,092		2,104	1,048	879	827	797	10
12	63.22	196.34	610	1,894	5,882	18,270	56,743		2,194	1,161	1,008	967	949	12
14	20.01	74.17	275	1,019	3,779	14,010	51,937		2,284	1,277	1,141	1,109	1,098	14
16	6.46	28.50	126	555	2,447	10,793	47,611		2,376	1,395	1,276	1,251	1,245	16
YEARS	65	55	45	35	25	15	5		5	15	25	35		

PUT IN AT ONE TIME to age 65

TAKE OUT MONTHLY from age 65

At age 30, it would take a one-time investment of $13,011 to accomplish your goal, using 6% compounded annually. That is, your $13,011 would need to compound at 6% a year for 35 years in order for you to TAKE OUT $560 each month from age 65 until you reached 100. In other words, at age 30 you would have PUT IN $13,011 at one time to TAKE OUT $235,200 between age 65 and 100.

If you waited only 10 years, to age 40, it would take $23,300 (or $10,289 more) to accomplish the same financial goal of receiving $560 each month.

If, on the other hand, you reached for a higher percentage rate (8% at age 30) you would find that $6,763 would give you $690 a month from age 65 to age 100. If you wanted to receive only $560 a month, the amount needed at age 30 at 8% is not $6,763 but only $5,489; i.e., ($6,763 ÷ $690) x $560 = $5,489. By realizing an 8% average annual rate of return instead of 6%, it would take only $5,489 instead of $13,011 (42% less).

Amazing Results Over Time

Obviously, the earlier you start, the less money it takes.

It is interesting to observe that at age 20, IF you could obtain a 10% annual rate of return on your money and IF you PUT IN AT ONE TIME $1,372 and allowed it to compound until age 65 (45 years), you could TAKE OUT $827 each month or a total of $347,340 from age 65 to age 100. Subtracting the amount you PUT IN from the amount you could TAKE OUT, shows that the total amount of income you would receive would be $345,968 over and above what you invested.

The tables in this chapter illustrate the importance of reaching for the **highest average annual rate of return** you believe you can comfortably and securely receive on your investment. The higher the rate, the less money it takes to provide what you want, but the risk is higher too. **The**

importance of time is stressed in these tables. Obviously, the earlier you start, the less money it takes.

The preceding tables are mathematical compound interest computations, and do not refer to any particular type of investment. Furthermore, they do not take taxes or the loss in value of a dollar over time into consideration. They are shown to give you an idea of how much money it would take at various average annual rates of return and over various periods of time to accomplish your financial goals. They also show dramatically the power of compounding and the tremendous importance of what we all have so little of...TIME. They indicate how important it is for you to **utilize time to your best advantage.**

The Four Keys to Accumulating Wealth

In conclusion, the following points should be quite clear:

1. **Start investing as early as possible. It takes significantly less money to accomplish what you want, and you have more time working for you.**

2. **Be determined to save on a regular basis. It is an easy way to accumulate wealth.**

3. **Begin investing with the largest possible sum you can. You will have more money working for you over a longer period of time.**

4. **Reach for the highest rate of return you believe you can safely receive on your money over time. Each additional percent is important. The higher the rate, the less money it takes to accomplish what you want.**

If you would like to study additional tables about the compounding of money, turn to Addendum A.

Confronting Your Financial Challenges

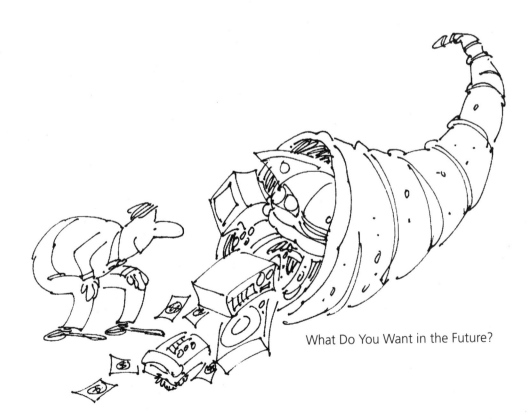

What Do You Want in the Future?

What Do You Want in the Future?

Salud, pesetas, y amor, y tiempo para gozarlos.

"Health, wealth and love – and time to enjoy them" is an ancient Spanish proverb that best describes the idea that **money has no value unless one has the time and good health to enjoy it.**

Consider:

If you **have to be poor,** would you rather be poor **now** or **at retirement?**

Do you feel confident that **someone else** is going to take care of you if you have a financial problem?

Do you want to try to control your own destiny rather than be controlled by circumstances?

Can you commit yourself to putting order into your life so that you can accomplish your goals?

You can become financially independent – if you have enough time remaining and **if** you have the determination to achieve your goals.

Your purpose in life is not to save; it is to be able to do what you want to do. Unfortunately, you can't have everything. You must decide what you want the most and then make plans to acquire it. The most important step is to set priorities and then search for the means by which you can achieve your goals.

You can determine the course of your life. Financial independence is one of the means by which you can do what you want to do when you want to do it.

As you travel through life in pursuit of financial independence, you may feel it is a long journey full of obstacles. However, after you travel

...after you travel
life's road and look
back, that same path
looks very short.

life's road and look back, that same path looks very short. You will wonder how the time could have passed so quickly.

What Challenges Do You Face?

Consider where you are today, then step back and look at some of the challenges you will face in the future:

Making a living
Keeping your job
Saving enough/not spending too much
Deciding where savings should be invested
Getting your money's worth
Providing for education
Maintaining your health
Providing for a catastrophe (emergency reserve)
Staying out of debt
Keeping up with the Joneses
Providing for child and parent care
Living too long
Dying too soon

If you are young, you may want to live a full life in a hurry. You have to have a car just as soon as you get your first job; you don't believe you can do without it. Even when just starting out, you may desire a home of your own. Probably you want all the trappings of the good life before you have really established yourself. Indeed, many of us are ready for retirement with the sound of the opening gun.

Indeed, many of us are ready for retirement with the sound of the opening gun.

Delaying what you want **now** in order to achieve financial independence in the future may not seem like much fun. Being thrifty may be something foreign to you. If your guiding principle is to satisfy as many wants as possible in the shortest time, you may not wish to put off until tomorrow what you can get on credit today. Sometimes your only restraints are those imposed by your finance company or bank.

For many of us, life unfolds this way: As we get older and our income increases, we may have extra money to spend, allowing us to reach a little higher standard of living. We move from our first home to a better one and surround ourselves with luxuries that reflect an

Sometimes your only restraints are those imposed by your finance company or bank.

...face the financial
realities of life.

increased income. We are not overly concerned about the future. We are confident that when the time comes, we will make sufficient money to provide what we want. The possibility that we might become physically unable to work or might have business reversals does not seem to dampen our optimism or curb our spending. As we move along in our careers, we see misfortunes happening to others, but we believe they won't happen to us.

This pattern can continue through our working years unless we are brought down to earth by circumstances to face the financial realities of life.

Special Challenges to Consider:

- **Getting Ahead**
- **Deciding on Your Most Important Wants**
- **Living Within Your Means**
- **Becoming Aware of Money Management**

- **Getting Ahead**

To earn money, most of us learn certain skills and apply them to a job. We try to be successful by learning and becoming more proficient. It takes a great deal of time, thinking, planning, determination and study to develop additional skills. But having a set of skills is not enough. We must apply them.

Financial success is seldom an accident. Prosperity almost always comes from hard work and saving over time. If you want to succeed financially, **wishing cannot replace working**. You must be determined to accomplish your goal.

◆ Deciding on Your Most Important Wants

As you earn money, you face another financial challenge. How should you use it?

Few people have unlimited resources. You bring home a certain amount and no more. This is all the money you have to work with each month. After federal, state, local and Social Security taxes, there is only a certain amount left for all of your wants. Most of us have more wants than we have income to provide them. This creates the challenge of deciding which want has priority. As soon as you realize that there isn't enough money to have everything you would like, you can prioritize your wants. You may learn that **if you spend all of your money for a particular want, none will be left for the others**. You may also learn, perhaps the hard way, that if you spend more money than you earn, you will run out of money.

Most of us have more wants than we have income to provide them. This creates the challenge of deciding which want has priority.

Since **money can be spent (traded) only once**, you need to decide which wants are the most important. To do this, it may be helpful to place a personal value on each of your wants and rank them in order of priority. Some items on your list might be:

WANTS	VALUE TO YOU
Fancy home	Satisfying a dream
Jacuzzi	Feeling good
Stereo and video system	Entertainment
Designer clothes	Being stylish
Sports car	Fulfilling a childhood desire
Vacation home	Relaxing
Boat	Sailing, fishing
Country club	Socializing, sports and prestige
Video camera	Recording experiences
Air conditioning	Being comfortable
Swimming pool	Exercising, pleasure and status
Education for children	Providing them with a good start in life
Saving and investing	Achieving financial independence

Once you decide how to spend your income, you must also make sure you get your money's worth. **This is a real challenge**. Should you buy a cheaply-made item and possibly be forced to replace it, or should you pay more for a quality item that will last? In the long run, which is the best trade for your money?

◆ Living Within Your Means

You can easily over-extend yourself using credit. You can raise your current standard of living to such a high level that it cannot be sustained. For example, if you buy a big home, a car, furniture and major appliances on credit, you obligate yourself to making large monthly payments for many months into the future. **You are committing yourself today to the way you will spend your future income.** If your monthly payments and your current living expenses are greater than your income, you are in serious financial difficulty.

Forgetting You Have Money Saved

You may need to make a conscious effort to forget you have money saved. Each time you remember you have money, you may think of a way to spend it. In order to save money, you must fight to keep from spending it.

Believing You Can Run Out of Money

In order to save money, you must fight to keep from spending it.

As you age, the scales tend to shift sides. Instead of having the desire to spend money, you want to save. **You face a new challenge – the fear of running out of money**. You may be afraid that if you die too soon, your family could run out of money. Likewise, if you live too long and are unable to work, **you** may run out of money.

How much money will it take to
provide what you really want?

◆ Becoming Aware of Money Management

You may not fully understand money and how to manage it effectively, even though you **are aware** of the fundamental concepts of the importance of time and of the eroding value of a dollar.

You may not know:

How much money it will take to provide what you really want.

How much money you will need each month **for the rest of your life.**

How much money you may need for care **if you become disabled.**

How much money it will take in one lump sum to provide what you want your survivors to have **if you die.**

You may be unaware that:

What you are doing now may not accomplish your financial goals.

Managing money is just as important as earning it.

You could be paying too much for life insurance, or that you could be under-insured.

Why might you be unaware? You simply may not take enough time to collect the facts or to think them through; you may be too busy. You have no time to stop and think about your future, because all of your time is spent worrying about the challenges of surviving day to day.

There is another reason. You might be an expert in your own profession, but no one can be an **expert at everything**. Perhaps all of your time is spent trying to be successful in your profession; therefore, you may not have the extra time to become an expert in financial matters as well. You may not realize that managing money is just as important as earning it.

You may not realize that managing money is just as important as earning it.

We have covered some of the financial challenges you might face in the future. Taken as a whole, it may appear that you are up against an impossible task. **The solution to big problems is like a statue buried in a large block of stone. The shape of the solution lies somewhere inside the stone. By chipping at it a little piece at a time, with great patience and care, you will eventually uncover the final image.**

The problem solver is you. **YOU have many assets and, hopefully, good health working for you.** You also have the ability to learn, and the strength to continue to earn.

You will never have more time remaining than you have RIGHT NOW.

The time you have remaining in your life is also a precious asset. You will never have more time remaining than you have RIGHT NOW.

Take a Personal Inventory

Which of these personal assets do you have?

Physical:
> Appearance
> Energy
> Health
> Time remaining

Mental:
> Intelligence
> Creativity
> Ability to adapt and to learn

Emotional:
> Enthusiasm
> Determination
> Self-esteem
> Positive attitude
> Confidence

Professional:
> Education
> Experience
> Knowledge
> Skills and talents

Social:
> Friends and associates
> Family

Understanding and using your unique characteristics to your advantage will help you greatly in determining your financial future. Your awareness of your strengths and weaknesses will motivate you to make improvements over time.

One of the most important assets, besides your continued good health and your time remaining, will be **your determination** – a persistent desire to constantly improve yourself that is one of the most important steps in becoming financially independent.

Understanding and using your unique characteristics to your advantage will help you greatly in determining your financial future.

Taking a personal inventory.

Planning for Daily Wants

Planning for Daily Wants

*If you spend more than you make,
   you are spending your future income.*

Planning to Live Within Your Income

It takes more than love, food, clothing and shelter to have a satisfactory life. Transportation, education, health care and entertainment help make life more complete.

Your tastes and priorities determine the number and costs of your wants. As long as the total cost of the items you purchase is less than the income you bring home, you are "living within your income." The more money you save before paying for your wants, the better prepared you will be to face future financial storms and the more money you will have to invest in your financial independence. **In order not to spend more than you make, you must plan and be disciplined and determined.**

If you spend more than you make, you are spending your future income. You are committing money you haven't yet earned. You are taking on a future obligation. If these commitments are monthly installment payments, you are obligating yourself to earn even more money in the future so that you can repay what you have already spent. If you spend more than you earn, you must use borrowed money to do it. Unfortunately, our society and, specifically, financial institutions encourage the use of credit – in other words, borrowing.

It takes more than love, food, clothing and shelter to have a satisfactory life.

The Credit Card Trap

The use of charge accounts became popular years ago as a convenient way to pay for purchases made during a month. Over time, the businesses that offered charge accounts found that many people spent more than they earned and were unable to pay the full balance of what they owed at the end of the month. At first, some businesses reacted by cancelling the accounts. Others, however, took advantage of the situation and turned the unpaid balances into loans, charging high interest rates to compensate for the higher risk and the lack of collateral. As a consequence, financial institutions began issuing credit cards. Some people consider charge accounts and credit cards a convenience, but for many their use is a dangerous financial trap. Adopting a policy of **cash only** can prevent you from falling into such a trap.

The Credit Card Trap

What if you have already fallen into the credit card trap? What options do you have?

One option is to spend some time talking with your local banker. Learn if your banker would loan you the amount of your credit card balance so that you could repay the credit card company. Your banker will consider your credit rating, the quality of any of your collateral you offer and your ability to repay the loan. Provided your banker is willing to loan money to you, the interest rate that the bank would charge would likely be **much** lower than that charged by the credit card company. After repaying your credit card balance, then make a solemn vow never to fall into that trap again.

The second option you have, is to bring your unpaid balance down to zero as fast as you can. If you are making other investments as you are paying down your credit card loan, stop. Take some time to rethink this. Can you afford to continue this investment? Can you afford to invest at the same time you are in the credit card trap? Ask yourself, are you absolutely assured you will earn 18% on your investments? If you are not sure, why not concentrate all of your effort on paying down your credit card balance as fast as you can, rather than making other investments? The credit card company is charging you 18% now. **By paying down your credit card balance, isn't that the same thing as earning 18% on your money?**

Get rid of your credit card.

Two Basic Reasons to Borrow Money

Borrowing to invest – If we didn't borrow money to buy a home, most of us would not be able to own one. A home provides a place to live that is also an investment because it offers the potential for growth in value.

Borrowing to consume – Although many people think a new car is an investment, this is generally not true because it loses value too rapidly. In reality, if you borrow money to buy a car you are actually borrowing to consume. In our country, a car is almost a necessity. **There is nothing wrong with buying a car, but why not buy one for which you can afford to pay cash?**

Hidden Obligations

Simply possessing or using certain things may require you to commit future dollars. For example, if you trade money for a camera, you commit future cash for film and processing costs. When you trade money to purchase a car, you commit yourself to paying for taxes, insurance, gasoline, parking and repairs. In addition, you lose the earnings on the assets tied up in your car while its value decreases with age. Similarly, when you trade money for a home, you commit to making monthly payments and to paying taxes and insurance premiums. You also trade dollars for furnishings, light, heat, cooling and maintenance. **That is, you have committed the use of part of your future earnings. In other words, it often costs more than the purchase price to own something.**

Having Second Thoughts

Before we were married, my future wife, Virginia, who was just out of nursing school wanted to buy a car. She received money from her father for a car and asked me to help her find a good used one. I asked her whether she would be able to afford all the other expenses that went with owning a car if she bought one. After thinking about it, she deferred the purchase, returned the money to her father, and found she was able to manage by walking and riding the bus.

Before buying your next car, consider the options. Do you want to live within your income, prioritize your wants and pay cash for transportation? Or do you want to borrow money to buy a car and obligate your future earnings?

The point of this example is that **if you want to achieve financial independence, you must plan and be disciplined and determined to control your wants**. You don't want to find yourself buying things that cost more than you expect (due to their upkeep) or **mortgaging your future** by spending more than you make, especially if you cannot afford the extra expense.

If you don't have enough money to buy what you want, why borrow money to buy it now? Why not wait until you **can** afford it? Why not make up your mind that you will never borrow money for anything you intend to consume, such as food, clothing and transportation? Can you live within your income? The answer is "yes" if you decide not to buy until you have the money.

If you don't have enough money to buy what you want, why borrow money to buy it now?

Planning for Emergencies

Planning for Emergencies

If you don't provide for your emergencies, who will?

Life is full of risks and financial pitfalls. As an income earner, you must consider the unpleasant possibility that something may happen to affect your earning ability. This would impact your current lifestyle and deter you from achieving your financial goals. In some respects, the world in which we live can be hazardous to our financial health. In planning our future, it would be wise to take into account the consequences of these risks.

The world in which we live can be hazardous to our financial health.

For the sake of simplicity, these risks can be divided into three categories: Personal, Property and Business.

Personal Risks

Health
    Short-term disability
    Long-term disability

Accident
    Temporary disability
    Permanent disability

Property Risks		**Business Risks**
Fire	Nature	Termination
Accidents	Earthquake	Business failure
Home	Hurricane	Strike
Car	Storms (tornado,	
Robbery	lightning, flood, etc.)	

The probability of you facing the consequences of many of these risks is remote, and the likelihood of a number of them happening in a short period is extremely remote. **But any one of them could happen to you.**

Should any of these events occur, however, a considerable amount of money might be required to meet expenses. There also might be other risks unique to your special occupation. If something **does** happen, you should be prepared to cope with it. Do you want to be in control, or are you willing to be at the mercy of unforeseen events?

Your Emergency Reserve

There also might be
risks unique to your
special occupation.

Your first priority should be to build an emergency reserve. You may be advised it would be wise to set aside between three and six months of living expenses in easily accessible savings. If you are not working or if you are planning to retire, you may wish to transfer some of your long-term assets to your emergency reserve, increasing it to six months or more. The amount of your emergency reserve may vary according to the flexibility of your budget and your comfort zone. Bear in mind that these liquid assets are there to see you through financial storms while you maintain a long-term strategy to protect the value of other investments.

Your emergency reserve is not intended to cover all possible risks. For complete protection, including such things as long-term disability and fire protection, you clearly need to have insurance.

When purchasing insurance, you can normally save a considerable amount on premiums by **using high deductibles,** which you can pay out of the emergency reserve if the need arises.

After you have decided the amount you want in your emergency reserve, consider where this reserve will be kept. Your reserve should be:

>**Readily available** on short notice (liquid)

>**Safe,** with the return of your money guaranteed or relatively assured

>**Income-producing**

Several options that meet all these criteria are:

>Banks

>Credit unions

>Savings and loans

>Money market mutual funds

The first three options are guaranteed. Money market funds are not. They are designed to return $1, plus interest, for every dollar invested, although there is no assurance that they will be able to do so. They are relatively safe investments.

Your choice of investment instruments should depend on their ease of access and how much safety they offer you.

Our Emergency Reserve

*During the early years of our marriage, we felt we could not afford to have a large fixed income emergency reserve. We believed we could not have so much money tied to the value of a dollar. We decided that about one month's living costs in reserve would be enough in our bank account. The rest of the assets were invested for the long term in mutual funds for our future financial security. **We actually considered our long-term investments as part of the emergency reserve;** that is, we could use them as collateral for a short-term loan – if the need arose. In fact, we needed to do that several times. **But we always had the means to pay back the loan at any time.***

3

Planning for Your Survivors

MY INTENT *in this section is to convey several fundamental messages for anyone who wishes to provide for a loved one. While there are many family lifestyles, this section takes a "case study" approach, assuming that you are a husband who wishes to provide for your wife, a research scientist. Recognizing the growing participation of women in business and as providers, the ideas and examples in the next three chapters (8, 9 and 10) can apply to anyone, male or female.*

How Much Money Is Needed?

How Much Money Is Needed?

*We all face the reality that we will die someday;
the only question is "when?"*

You are confident that, in one way or another, while you live you will be able to provide for yourself and your loved ones. However, what happens if you die prematurely? No one knows what the future has in store. Why not consider all the possibilities when planning your financial future? One of the possibilities is that you might die sooner than you expect. Should this happen, what challenges will your family face?

Final Expenses

First, there would be certain final expenses: medical and funeral expenses, estate taxes and perhaps probate costs.

Medical expenses vary widely, depending on the length of your illness and insurance coverage. The costs can be shockingly high and, unless you die quickly, they also can be overwhelming.

Funeral expenses, which vary from one area of the country to another, can be determined by inquiring at a funeral home. A traditional burial averages $4,600, while a cemetery plot and headstone can boost the cost by thousands more.

No one knows what the future has in store.

The federal government imposes an estate tax on that portion of your estate which exceeds $675,000 after deducting such matters as funeral expenses, debts, a marital deduction and charitable gifts. This estate tax exemption will rise to $1,000,000 by the year 2006. In addition, most states impose inheritance taxes. The exemptions and taxable rates vary from state to state.

Settling an estate through probate court can be costly, but the impact of estate taxes and probate costs can often be reduced by efficient estate planning and by **having a current will.** Obviously, the services of a competent attorney would be beneficial in this regard.

If you knew you were going to die tomorrow, you would be faced with at least two other related financial challenges **today:** first, to provide enough cash to take care of your survivors, and second, to make provisions for money management.

How Much Money Is Needed to Provide for Your Survivors' Future?

Before you can answer this question, consider:

- **What do you want your family to have?**

- **How much income is needed each month?**

- **Where can this money come from?**

- **How much cash is required today to provide the extra income for the future?**

◆ What do you want your family to have?

Do you want to provide your family with the same standard of living they are accustomed to? Do you want them to be able to remain in the same neighborhood? If you have children, do you want them to attend the same schools? Do you want them to have the college education you had planned? The answers are important, because they will help you determine what you want your family to have if you should die unexpectedly.

◆ How much income is needed each month?

To determine the monthly amount for your survivors, certain assumptions must be made. First, assume living costs will be the same in the future as they are today (these costs can be adjusted later).

Second, assume your family will continue to live in the same home. There are enough variables without changing homes.

How do you estimate the income it will take? First, determine how much it costs each month for you and your family to live. Of course, if you were to die tomorrow, some of the expenses would be reduced. For example, the food and clothing bills would be less and, most likely, the dental and medical bills would be reduced.

If you have children, money will probably be needed for their college education. The average tuition, room and board for college at a state university in 1998 was nearly $7,800 a year. Over a four-year period, this amounts to approximately $31,000 (in today's dollars) for each child. Private schools are much more expensive, averaging four times as much.

If you have children, money will be needed for their college education.

◆Where can this money come from?

The income you want your survivors to have can come from several sources, including:

Social Security benefits
Interest on savings
Income from investments
Insurance annuity income
Your spouse's salary
Family aid

If you have dependent children, Social Security benefits will make a good foundation for their support. In most cases, however, this income is not enough to meet all living and educational expenses, so one or more of the above sources must be tapped.

Stowers Financial Analysis

I have been asked, "What is the most important advice you can give people who are absolutely determined to improve their financial position?" My answer is, "I believe **nothing is more important** *than taking the time now, to learn exactly how much money it will take to provide what you want financially if you live, or what it will take in one lump sum, to provide for your loved one if you should die now."*

The information you are seeking can be found in a unique PC program, the Stowers Financial Analysis CD, which is included along with this book. The analysis is just as simple or as complicated as you want it to be.

Why not take time now to try this analysis?

From this program you will become aware of your exact future financial challenges. When you become aware of the extent of your challenges, the results will motivate you to determine exactly **what you want to do** to accomplish what you want and determine **when you want to do it.**

Think, **who will take care of you financially, if you don't?**

Who will be responsible for taking care of you?

My Experience

*Years ago, I asked myself these same questions. Who will take care of me financially? And if I didn't, who should be responsible for taking care of me? I asked myself if my relatives should do it. Should my kids be forced to take care of me? What about the government? Should I count on them? After a great deal of soul searching, I determined that **I was personally responsible for taking care of myself financially – no one else.***

Family Values

My father died many years ago. My mother remained a widow. Early on, I felt that my mother hesitated spending money for things she truly wanted so that there would be assets remaining for her two sons. My brother and I kept reminding my mother that she should do whatever she wanted to do, that her assets were hers, not ours. We certainly appreciated her thought about leaving assets for us, but we thought it was our responsibility to provide for our financial futures, not hers.

No one knows what the future has in store – each of us must understand the options available to protect our loved ones, and decide what is the best course to take.

In most cases the best insurance policy
for you is the least profitable for the agent.

Where Can the Money Come From?

The best insurance may well be the least expensive.

In the event of your death, a good source of extra money for your family can come from **Pure Permanent Annual Renewable Term Life Insurance**. Because it costs relatively little today to buy all the protection you want, there is no need to be under-insured. Insurance need not be expensive if you buy the right kind– that is, if you get your money's worth.

Life Insurance

In a time when millions of people spend billions on life insurance, it is startling how few have any real understanding of what they are buying and what they should expect from their insurance.

This lack of knowledge can be explained partially by the reliance on a life insurance agent for facts. In addition to performing a service for you, the agent has an interest in selling a policy and earning a commission. The higher the cost of a policy, the greater the company's profit and the higher the commission paid to the agent. In most cases, the best insurance policy for you is the least profitable for the agent.

Insurance companies are under no legal requirement to disclose all the facts. Policies are almost always sold as a package – a certain face dollar amount for a certain premium. You are seldom informed about how much of your premium payment goes to the agent as commission, how much is going to the company and how much is being spent for actual insurance protection. This is unlike the securities industry which is required by the government to provide full disclosure of important facts, including all costs and commissions.

Insurance policies are almost always sold as a package.

If you clearly understand the concept of when you need life insurance, how much and what kind gives you the most protection for your money, and how long you need to keep it, you do not have to be told by anyone what you should or should not do. But what if you don't fully understand the concept?

When Should You Buy Life Insurance?

If you are not worried about the consequences of dying prematurely, why waste **any** of your money on life insurance?

The odds are good that you **will live** beyond 65. If you are confident that you will exceed that age, why carry any insurance? Why not cancel all of your life insurance policies? If you are not worried about dying, why waste your money on life insurance? Why pay any premiums at all? Why not use the money to "live a little" today and enjoy life more?

You would probably say, "I can't do that – I might die before then." So ask yourself – "**when** might I die?" This is one of the most important questions that you must ask yourself. Be fair, and answer it rationally.

Look at **your life line** in the chart below, and check off the time you believe that you might die. Take time now to determine your **end of the line**.

(9-1)   *Your Life Line*

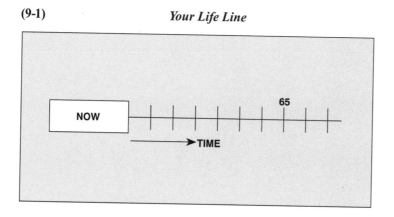

Again, if you are not worried about dying until 10 years from today, why carry any life insurance now? Why not drop all of your policies, save money, and stack those dollars on top of one another for your future? Aren't there more enjoyable ways of spending your money? Just before your **end of the line**, why not buy a huge policy and leave your family well off?

When should you buy life insurance?

Again, you will no doubt say, "I can't do that...I might die before then." But when? Aren't you carrying life insurance **now** because you are worried that you might die **tonight** – not 10 years in the future or at age 65 – but **tonight**? If you understand this concept, you will never have any difficulty deciding **when** you should have insurance on your life.

Let's illustrate this point in another, less emotional way – using **fire insurance**, something most of us buy wisely.

You have the fire insurance because you are worried that you might have a fire tonight, not five or 10 years in the future, but tonight.

If you own a home you carry fire insurance, don't you? You don't believe your house will burn to the ground – but it **could** happen. You have the fire insurance because you are worried that you might have a fire **tonight**, not five or 10 years in the future, but tonight. **Why not carry the same reasoning over to your consideration of life insurance**?

The First Year of Our Marriage

During the first few months of our marriage, my wife and I wondered if I should have life insurance to protect her if I died and, if so, how much. At the time, I was 30 years old and had one $10,000 policy on my life which my mother had purchased several years earlier. We determined life insurance was not needed, because of the money we had saved and invested. We were both unwilling to pay the $210 premium due on the existing policy. It was better to invest the $210 each year than spend it on life insurance. We terminated the policy and gave the cash value of $900 back to my mother.

We decided it was wiser to buy a large amount of life insurance when we had children. Therefore, when we were expecting *our first child in 1956, we bought $200,000 worth of life insurance on my life. Ordinary life insurance for $200,000 would have cost us $3,200 in annual premiums. Instead we bought annual renewable term insurance with a premium cost of only $926 each year. The term policy provided the most protection for the least amount of money and saved us $2,274 that year alone ($3,200 - $926 = $2,274). (More about annual renewable term insurance later.)*

Assets Needed for Survivors' Security

The bottom line in the following chart is drawn to represent your LIFE LINE. It begins with NOW at the left and extends into your future toward the right. Above this line is drawn your Survivors' Security Line. This represents the assets needed, in the event of your death, to provide your family with the necessary income. It is highest NOW and decreases as time passes. For example, 10 years from today, your children will be 10 years older, 10 years further through school, 10 years closer (you hope) to being self-supporting. Your spouse will be 10 years older and will have 10 years' worth of living expenses already paid. For these reasons, the need for Survivors' Security decreases with each passing year.

(9-2)   *Assets Needed for Survivors' Security*

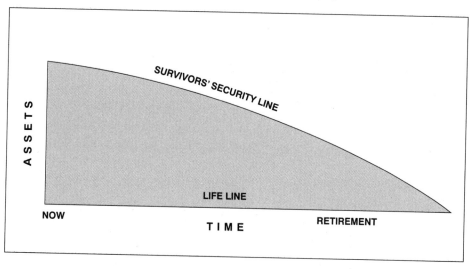

On the other hand, your goal of being financially independent is separate and distinct from your Survivors' Security. In the next chart, your LIFE LINE is again drawn from NOW into your future. Above your LIFE LINE is your Financial Independence Line. This represents the total assets you plan to accumulate in the future for yourself and your family. You want the amount to increase from NOW, so that you will achieve your goal of being financially independent at retirement. This is your own goal... **to be financially independent**.

(9-3)   *Assets You Accumulate... Toward Financial Independence*

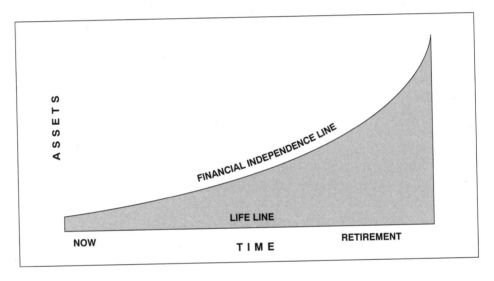

If you superimpose your Survivors' Security Line over your Financial Independence line, you can clearly visualize how much extra money is needed to provide for your family in the event of your death today.

As Chart 9-4 indicates, in the event of your premature death, a portion of the money your family will need can come from the assets you already have accumulated. Initially, though, most of it will probably have to come from life insurance or from some other outside source.

As time passes, your Survivors' Security Line decreases, while your Financial Independence Line (your accumulated assets) increases. The darker shaded area indicates the total amount of extra money you need for your survivors' security beyond the amount you have already accumulated. That extra amount indicates the amount of insurance you should probably have. As you can see, the amount of insurance necessary to provide for your Survivors' Security decreases with the passage of time.

(9-4) *The Extra Assets Needed*

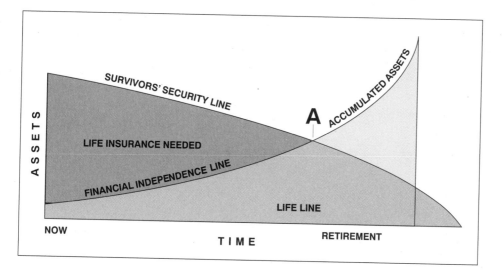

When point A in the chart above is reached, the assets you have accumulated are exactly equal to the amount of money you want for your survivors' security. At this point, you are fully **self-insured** through **your own** investments. Accordingly, there is no need for any outside insurance money from that point on. Instead of wasting money on life insurance premiums from Point A until your retirement, why not invest all of the premiums in order to reach your financial goal earlier? This could mean an earlier retirement or more luxurious lifestyle for your family. But until you reach Point A, you will probably need some insurance to protect your family.

If you knew you
were going to
die tonight…

If you knew you were going to die tonight:

	ANSWER
When would you buy life insurance?	Now
How much life insurance would you buy?	As much as I could
How much would you be willing to pay?	Least amount possible

According to some insurance agents, you have one reason for buying insurance, while your neighbor, who is the same age, has quite a different reason. For $1,000 worth of protection you are convinced to pay one price, your neighbor another. For the same amount of insurance at age 35, one of you pays an annual premium of $2.43, the other, an annual premium of $60. If both of you die, your survivors will receive a check for the same amount of money, $1,000. The higher the premium, the more the protection costs. The only difference in the amount you pay depends upon how informed you are and what **you are willing to pay** for the same life insurance benefit.

The notion that the higher the premium, the greater the protection, is not necessarily true. Assuming all insurance companies have the same financial stability, **the best insurance may well be the least expensive**.

There is one type of policy that gives you the most protection for the least amount of money. It offers protection only – no savings or cash value – only pure insurance. This is one of the policies used by life insurance companies when they buy and sell insurance among themselves. This is the **Pure Permanent Annual Renewable Term** life insurance policy. It is **pure** because it provides only insurance protection; it is not an investment since it has no cash value. It is **permanent** because the insurance is guaranteed renewable for life. Your actual cost for this insurance rises along with the expected mortality cost to the life insurance company. Most other life insurance policies have much higher costs each year **for life**. The premium rate of the policy is determined by adding an expense and profit factor to the cost derived from the life insurance mortality table. **As the mortality cost increases, so does the premium rate necessary for that age** (i.e., the older you get, the greater probability that you are going to die).

(9-5)   *Premium Rates for each $1,000 of Insurance*

Pure Permanent Annual Renewable Term

Attained Age	Premium per $1,000	Attained Age	Premium per $1,000	Attained Age	Premium per $1,000	Attained Age	Premium per $1,000
20	$1.73	40	$3.42	60	$19.66	80	$106.27
21	1.77	41	3.72	61	21.49	81	115.32
22	1.80	42	4.03	62	23.49	82	124.81
23	1.83	43	4.38	63	25.68	83	134.67
24	1.85	44	4.76	64	28.06	84	144.94
25	1.87	45	5.17	65	30.68	85	155.70
26	1.90	46	5.64	66	33.57	86	166.98
27	1.93	47	6.15	67	36.76	87	178.87
28	1.97	48	6.72	68	40.28	88	191.55
29	2.01	49	7.35	69	44.07	89	205.28
30	2.06	50	8.04	70	48.11	90	220.43
31	2.12	51	8.81	71	52.32	91	237.46
32	2.18	52	9.63	72	56.67	92	256.94
33	2.25	53	10.53	73	61.13	93	279.52
34	2.32	54	11.50	74	65.82	94	305.95
35	2.43	55	12.57	75	70.89	95	339.36
36	2.56	56	13.73	76	76.51	96	387.02
37	2.71	57	15.02	77	82.87	97	471.90
38	2.91	58	16.43	78	89.92	98	645.56
39	3.15	59	17.97	79	97.77		

The premium rates in the chart above are from a policy issued by our Survivors' Benefit Insurance Company which we sold in 1980. These rates are comparable to rates that can be found with other life insurance companies today. Notice how slowly the premiums rise from year to year.

The premium rates for $1,000 worth of insurance are graphed to scale in the chart below. Superimposed upon this graph is an appropriate **Need for Protection** line.

(9-6)   *Annual Renewable Term Life Insurance*

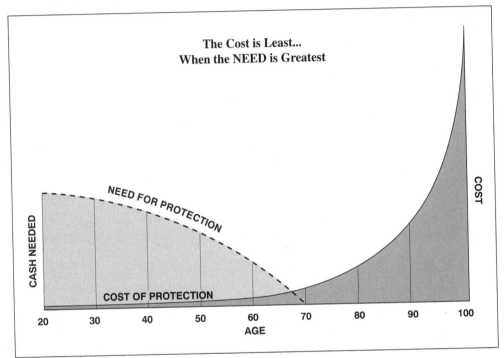

The cost goes up each year **along with** the mortality cost on a very gradual basis. **The cost of protection is least, when the need for it is greatest**.

Annual renewable term life insurance can be described as a **"pay-as-you-go, get-what-you-pay-for"** policy. If you are 35 years old, you are not required to pay today the higher cost required at age 60 or even age 36. You can pay that higher rate **if and when** you arrive at that age.

Who buys annual renewable term life insurance? Usually there are only three groups of people who do:

Those who completely understand insurance.

Those who have limited funds and cannot afford expensive insurance.

Those who are getting their money's worth without knowing it.

For current information on premium rates and insurance companies, please visit our website at www.stowers-innovations.com.

Money Management

Money Management

*The biggest challenge of money management
is how to make money with money.*

Even if you are able to provide your survivors with the cash they
will need, is this all you need to do?

In the case of death, either spouse may be faced with difficult financial decisions. For the purposes of illustration, the following example
assumes that the wife has been widowed. Besides taking care of the
funeral arrangements, taxes, doctor bills, calming herself and reassuring
the family, your widow will be contacted by a representative of one of
your insurance companies. Actually, she doesn't want to talk to anyone,
but the financial situation demands it.

*Even if you are able
to provide your
survivors with the
cash they will need,
is this all you need
to do?*

The agent tells your widow how much insurance you provided for
her. He asks her what she wants to do with the money. Not being sure
what to do, she asks the agent for advice. The agent suggests an insurance annuity that would pay her a definite sum each month for the rest
of her life. "The money will never run out," the agent says, and encour-
ages her to do this. Because she is upset and does not want to make any
major financial decisions quickly, she tells the agent she wants to think
about it. At this point, she is not certain what she should do. She is anxious
and confused.

Next, she might seek advice from close friends. They might explain
that an insurance annuity is not the answer because it does not protect
her against future inflation. They tell her there will be no way to obtain
additional cash in case of an emergency. Instead of an insurance annuity,
they recommend that she take all the money from the insurance company and deposit it in several different savings and loan associations.
They feel she will earn more money from her investment that way. She
listens to what they say, but is still undecided.

Your widow tells your doctor about her financial problems and asks advice.

Perhaps your family doctor calls on your widow. During the conversation, she tells your doctor about her financial problems and asks advice. The doctor advises her to invest in mutual funds and let professionals manage the money.

This sounds logical but she is not ready to make financial decisions, and she continues to seek advice.

An enterprising broker reads of your death and contacts your widow. Again, she solicits advice. The broker suggests she take the money in cash and permit him to invest it, indicating that her problems will then be solved. She will have no more decisions to make; they will be made for her. But she still has questions.

While discussing the settlement of your estate with her attorney, your widow reveals her problem. The attorney suggests that she create a trust and allow a bank trust department to administer it for her.

No wonder your widow is confused. Everyone she has talked with has given her different advice. She feels that some of her advisers are looking out for their own best interests. She realizes that this might be the largest lump sum of money she will ever receive, and she is afraid of making the wrong decision and losing money. Because she remains confused, she does nothing. She tells the insurance company to pay the money to her in cash. She deposits the money in her checking account and then waits, hoping that somehow a decision will be made for her.

Several years later, your widow confides in a close friend: "I am worried about my money. I am not sure what to do. **I wish my husband and I had discussed this while he was still alive.**"

Is providing enough money for your survivors all you should do? Of course not. Why not discuss your opinions with your spouse and make a plan together while you both are still alive?

Before you agree on a plan, why not first consider the challenges of money management? There are two fundamental issues:

- **Spending Money Wisely**
- **Making Money With Money**

◆ Spending Money Wisely

Most people spend money wisely, trying to get their money's worth. If you fall into this category, you do not have a problem. If you believe there may be a problem, perhaps you can control the amount of money that will be available to spend by your survivor by using a trust instrument or an insurance annuity.

Trust Instrument

If you are worried about your survivor's ability to manage the spending of money, or if you want to limit the amount of money that can be spent, you can have your attorney establish a trust instrument now. In this legal document, you can give a trustee the power to control the

If you are worried about your survivor's ability to manage the spending of money...

spending of the assets. The trustee can be an individual or the trust department of a bank. If a trust is used, your survivor will usually be given a fixed amount of money to spend but can ask for more in a financial crisis. The trustee will charge a fee for this non-investment management service. It should be pointed out that it is unlikely that a trustee will be willing to perform this service only. The trustee will most likely ask to be given the right to make investment decisions as well and charge an additional fee.

Advantage of having a trustee:

Impartial control of spending

Disadvantages of using a trustee:

Your survivor may be at the mercy of the trustee even as a co-trustee in the document. If additional money is needed, your survivor must try to convince the trustee. If additional funds are needed for anything, your survivor must, in a sense, "beg" for the money. (This could be avoided if the trust allowed discretionary withdrawals.)

You may think that the fee required by the trustee for this service is not reasonable. You're probably right.

Insurance Annuity

Another way to control the spending of money would be to have your survivor buy an insurance annuity. The annuity is a contract issued by a life insurance company that guarantees a specific monthly payment for life.

Advantages of an insurance annuity:

Your survivor will receive a fixed income each month for life.

Your survivor will not need to be worried about money management.

Disadvantages of an insurance annuity:

The annuity does not provide for protection against any loss in the value of a dollar.

No extra cash is available. If there were an emergency requiring extra cash, the money could not be obtained from the insurance company.

An insurance annuity is expensive. It takes a great deal of cash to provide a guaranteed monthly payment for life.

If your survivor dies early, the value of the estate will be reduced.

◆ Making Money With Money

The biggest challenge of money management is how to make money with money. To make money with money, many decisions must be made. Someone must decide **where** to put the money to work, **how much** should be put in any one place, and **when** the money should be taken out and placed somewhere else. And those decisions must be made continually.

The biggest challenge of money management is how to make money with money.

Let's examine just three choices concerning who can make these money management decisions:

Your Survivor

A Trust Department

A Fully-Managed Mutual Fund

Your Survivor Can Make Decisions

Your survivor can listen to the suggestions of others, read financial periodicals, then take chances with individual security investments. As with anyone making financial decisions, investment success will be a function of education, experience in money matters, and ability to make the correct decisions. You need to consider the potential anxiety level associated with this choice.

A Trust Department

If your survivor is not confident about making investment decisions, your survivor can go to a bank trust department for money management. For a fee, the trustee will perform this service. For additional fees, a trust department will perform other services.

Advantages of having a trust department make investment decisions:

Offers professional experience in money management.

Removes the responsibility of money management from your survivor's shoulders.

Makes investment decisions according to your instructions.

Detailed record keeping is provided.

One advantage of having a trust department manage your money is that... investment decisions are made according to your instructions.

Disadvantages of using a trust department to manage money:

Generally, a trust department can offer only part-time investment management. For example, let's assume a trust department has 500 individual trust accounts. Let's also assume that there are 10 trust officers to manage these accounts. If the accounts were divided equally, each of the officers would have 50 accounts. If a trust officer spends equal time on each of his 50 accounts during a year, each account will receive the equivalent of only five working days of personal investment management a year. Actually, the time may not be divided this way. The larger accounts will undoubtedly command more time and the smaller accounts will receive less time.

The quality of a trust department's work depends on several factors: first, upon the **ability** of the particular investment adviser, and second, upon how much **time** the trust officer spends with your survivor's trust account. No matter how intelligent the trust officer, the quality of work cannot be good unless adequate time is spent on the account.

The investment management given by a trust department is generally overly conservative. With the fear of continued erosion in the value of a dollar, this conservative stance could adversely affect long-term investment results.

The past investment record of individual trusts of a trust department is not generally available to the public.

A Fully-Managed Mutual Fund

If your survivor does not want to make the individual investment decisions, the money can be managed by a **fully-managed mutual fund**. This type of fund is one in which the investment manager is given the broadest authority possible at all times to use his best judgment in managing the fund's assets as to:

The past investment record of individual trusts of a trust department is generally not available to the public.

What to invest in.

How much to invest in a particular security.

How long to remain invested.

How much cash should be held if more attractive investments cannot be found.

Advantages of having a fully-managed mutual fund:

A fund provides full-time rather than part-time management.

More investment management is received for each dollar paid.

No matter if your account is big or small, all investors get the same attention from the fund's management.

All the manager's time is spent taking care of one portfolio of securities. More time is spent making investment decisions, so there is greater opportunity for better results.

Detailed record keeping is provided.

The performance record is public and the results are audited.

Disadvantages of a fully-managed mutual fund:

Most of these funds invest only in marketable securities. Because of this, closely held companies and personal real estate investments cannot be used since they are not marketable.

No individual investment advice is given since the mutual fund is managed for all fund investors.

Investment decisions cannot be made according to your instructions.

Test drive your financial plan.

"Test Drive" Your Financial Plan

If you believe that the trust department of a bank is the best place for your survivor's money to be managed after you are gone, tell your survivor **now**. If the trust department is good enough for your survivor, why isn't it also good enough for you? Why not give the bank's trust department a chance to manage your money today? See what the bank can do with it and at what cost. If you are not satisfied now, why should your survivor be satisfied later?

If you decide mutual funds can best serve your family's financial needs, discuss it with your loved one **now**. Tomorrow may be too late.

Try investing some of your money in selected mutual funds. See what the results are. Find out what other services are offered. See if you are satisfied with what mutual funds **can do for you now**. Your family will benefit in the future from the experiences you gain today.

Planning for Financial Independence

Introduction to Investing

Introduction to Investing

*There is no such thing as a perfectly safe investment,
   free from all risk.*

If you want the financial freedom in the future to do what you want to do when you want to do it, you must begin to trade your money for something that can grow in value over time and/or will generate income. **This is investing**.

When considering investing, most people think primarily of putting their money to work productively. They look to their assets to provide a source of independent income – a second income – separate from work income.

No person is free, in an economic sense, who does not have adequate investment income entirely unrelated to work. A person earning $100,000 a year, without a nickel in investments to show for it, has less freedom than a person who earns a moderate wage but who owns income-producing assets paying $10,000 annually.

No person is free, in an economic sense, who does not have adequate investment income entirely unrelated to work.

One of the prime objectives of a sound investment program is to place the responsibility for protecting your investment on someone else's shoulders – someone experienced in managing money.

Perhaps no one appreciates the need for having investment income without the responsibility of management more than the owner of a small business. The more successful the business, the more dependent it is on every ounce of the owner's energy. It is as though the owner has the proverbial tiger by the tail and dares not let go. Sooner or later, every small business owner comes to realize that the degree of genuine financial success that the owner can enjoy is best measured by the amount of assets that are invested in someone else's business, often through common stocks.

There is another significant reason why you should be interested in delegating the investment management function: you accumulate investments not only for your own benefit, but also for your survivors. To the extent that your investments require your personal supervision – your ideas, planning, and judgment – it may not be desirable to have them taken over by your survivors who are much less familiar than you are with managing them.

It may not be desirable to have your investments taken over by your survivors who are much less familiar than you are with managing them.

How Investments Can Earn Money:

Appreciation – The increase in value of assets such as stocks, bonds, commodities or real estate

Dividends – Income received as an owner of a business

Interest – Income received from lending your money

Capital Gains – Profits received from the sale of assets

Basic Attributes of Attractive Investments

Some of the basic attributes investors look for in an attractive investment include:

- **Professional Management**
- **Income Production**
- **Capital Growth Opportunity**
- **Availability in Convenient Amounts**
- **Ease of Transfer of Ownership**
- **Liquidity (ease of sale)**
- **Acceptability as Collateral for a Loan**
- **Limited Liability**
- **Inflation Hedge**

✦ Professional Management

Professional management means transferring the responsibility to someone who is qualified to free you of day-to-day, time-consuming research and decisions relating to investments so that you can continue to devote your efforts to succeed in your chosen work.

✦ Income Production

The investment provides the possibility of ongoing income payments without the sale of capital assets. For example, investing in diamonds is not a good choice because they would not produce income. Only by selling them could you receive cash.

✦ Capital Growth Opportunity

You may seek an investment vehicle that offers the opportunity for your investment to grow in value.

✦ Availability in Convenient Amounts

Can the investment be purchased in comparatively small amounts at different times, such as shares of common stocks, or does it require a substantial immediate investment, such as a home?

✦ Ease of Transfer of Ownership

It is desirable to be able to easily transfer your interest in your investment to someone else, whether by sale or gift. Your options are extremely limited if you do not have this privilege.

◆ Liquidity

You want an active public market for your investments so that, should you decide to sell, you do not have to seek out an individual buyer. The importance of liquidity cannot be overemphasized. One of the advantages of being a stockholder in a publicly owned corporation is marketability – the ability to readily sell your stock.

◆ Acceptability as Collateral

You may have a temporary need for funds to meet an emergency or to take advantage of an opportunity. You do not want to sell your investment but simply borrow against it. Naturally, the ease with which it may be used as collateral for a loan contributes to the attractiveness of your investment. If a ready market exists for it, the lender will probably act much more favorably.

◆ Limited Liability

Most people are reluctant to own an investment in which their liability extends beyond the amount of money they have invested.

◆ Inflation Hedge

Your investment should have a good likelihood of appreciating in value to an amount equal to or greater than the loss in value of a dollar, so that it will keep up with the ongoing increases in costs of goods and services.

The Risks of Investing

Nothing is safe in an absolute sense. To think otherwise is to fool oneself. For example, each of us can and should drive our car carefully, but this in itself does not rule out the possibility of an accident, because we cannot control the actions of other drivers on the road.

Likewise, **there is no such thing as a perfectly safe investment**. It is not possible to insulate your financial plan from the effects of national and world economic events. We are living in a dynamic, fast-moving age, and every economic change that occurs can affect us in our pocketbooks.

Smart people do not seek to avoid risks, but simply try to hold them within reasonable limits. **Progress is not possible without risk**. No one can expect success to be guaranteed fully and completely in advance. In fact, experience indicates that those who painstakingly attempt to avoid all financial risks, seeking only "sure" things, face the greatest risk of all – the shrinking value of a dollar.

The two major investment risks involved in the accumulation or conservation of capital are:

- **Loss of Principal**
- **Loss in the Value of Your Dollars**

There is no savings or investment plan that is not subject to loss on one or both of these possibilities.

Guarantees are only as good as the financial strength of the organization standing behind them.

- **Loss of principal** requires little explanation. Any form of savings that does not guarantee to return to you at least the same number of dollars initially saved, anytime you want it, involves the possibility of losing principal. Guarantees are only as good as the financial strength of the organization standing behind them.

- **Loss in the value of your dollars** occurs when a dollar buys fewer goods and services than it did at a previous time.

In summary… **A loss in dollar value is just as real as a loss of principal. In fact, over time, the shrinking value of your dollars can be your greater loss.**

No one knowingly makes an investment
with the objective of losing money.

Types of Investments

*No one knowingly makes an investment
with the objective of losing money.*

If you want to put your money to work, you can either lend it to others or you can trade your dollars to own something. If you put your money to work, how much should you expect to make on your investment? If you are not sure how much your money can earn, it is easy to find out. **Just try to borrow money.** See how much you will have to pay to borrow it. This is a good indication of how much you should receive for your money.

There is a marked difference between being a **lender** and an **owner**. Both lenders and owners invest dollars for the same basic purpose: to earn more dollars. Only the approach to the objective is different.

...put your money
to work...

"Lender" Investments

Your primary concern when you lend money is the safety of the loan. Will the borrower be able to pay you the interest on time and repay the obligation in full when it matures?

A secondary consideration is the amount of interest a borrower agrees to pay you for the use of your money.

Here are some examples of loan-type investments:

- ◆ **Savings Accounts** – When you establish a savings account, you actually lend money. The institution agrees to pay you a stipulated rate of interest on the funds and generally makes them available to you when you want them.

◆ **Bonds** – A bond is merely the evidence of a loan – an interest-bearing certificate issued by a government or business. When you buy a bond, you are in effect lending your money to an organization or a government which promises to pay you a specified sum (interest) on specific dates and pay back your loan at maturity.

About Municipal Bonds

Some people are excited about the opportunity of receiving tax-free income from municipal bonds. Little or no effort is focused on the quality of the assets that actually back the bonds which protect the municipal bond. When a person compares the quality of those assets with the quality of the assets that back U.S. Government Bonds, there is a definite difference. People must determine whether they are willing to take more risk in order to obtain the tax-free income.

Consider some of the things that are NOT ordinarily a concern to you as a lender:

◆ You are not concerned about **how** the funds will be used. It is true that you want the borrower's business to prosper so that he will be able to make the interest payments to you as they fall due and, ultimately, to repay the entire loan. But, beyond that, your concern as a lender ceases. Likewise, when receiving 5% on your money from a bank, you are not really concerned about whether the bank earns 2%, 4%, or 8% on the funds you have advanced.

◆ As a lender, you play the role of a spectator. As long as the borrower continues to honor the terms of the contract, you have no voice in the borrower's operation.

◆ Only when a borrower fails to fulfill the terms of a contract, for example, by not paying the interest or principal when due, are you given the right to take an active part in the borrower's affairs.

• In theory, you as a lender do not share in the success or the failure, profits or losses of the borrower. In actual practice, of course, the losses (if they are sufficiently severe) can adversely affect your financial position. The savings and loan disaster of recent years is an excellent example of such an event.

Again remember: **There is no such thing as a completely risk-free investment!**

"Owner" Investments

An owner is one who has acquired the title to real or personal property. Generally, as an owner, you are interested in the safety of your principal and the production of investment income. As an owner, you willingly assume a greater degree of risk than a lender does in return for certain advantages of ownership.

• Risks of Ownership

As an owner, you absorb any losses sustained by your investment. In the event of a business failure, for example, you stand last in line to recover any part of your investment. **All lenders must be paid first**.

As an owner, no one promises to pay you a return on your investment. There are no guarantees or assurances. When making an investment, you may calculate that it will pay a given income. This is purely a matter of personal judgment and is not supported by any contractual understanding. Whether or not the investment will return income to you depends entirely on the profits of the investment.

Profits are generally unpredictable. This is particularly true over extended periods of time. If you were to purchase an apartment building, it would be reasonable to assume that you could determine with some degree of accuracy your beginning gross income from rent after the expenses of servicing and maintaining the property. To make a projection of earnings five or 10 years into the future becomes increasingly more

...other factors beyond the home itself contribute to its selling price.

difficult. What can you expect the rents to be at that time? The rate of occupancy? The labor and maintenance costs? Real estate taxes? The variables that affect the level of profits are almost without end, and the attractiveness of your investment hinges on all these variables.

There is no guarantee of the value you will receive for the property if you choose to sell. If you invested $10,000 in U.S. government savings bonds or in a single-premium life insurance policy, you know precisely what the value of your investment is at any given time. If, however, you invested $10,000 in a retail business, you could not accurately predict what you would receive from the sale of the business.

The selling price you will receive for property at any given time depends not only on the worth of the investment itself, but also the uncertainties of the marketplace and on the value of a dollar at that time. For example, the structural integrity of a home clearly affects its value. But other factors beyond the home itself contribute to its selling price. For instance, what demand will exist for homes at the time you decide to sell? How popular will the neighborhood be? If you are required to sell at a time when market conditions are generally unfavorable, you may receive considerably less for the property than if the sale were held under more ideal conditions.

Direct ownership of real estate for investment purposes fails to satisfy many of the basic attributes of attractive investments:

♦ **As a real estate owner, you cannot completely free yourself from management responsibilities. Although you may delegate certain responsibilities to an agent, you will always be expected to make the important decisions.**

- **Direct ownership of real estate is not available in small denominations. While it is true that you can arrange for a small down payment, financing the balance with a mortgage, you are usually required to make a substantial initial investment.**

- **Real estate suffers from a lack of guaranteed marketability.**

◆ Advantages of Ownership

The factors that are responsible for putting you as an owner at a disadvantage under adverse conditions also give you a powerful advantage when conditions are favorable.

An owner receives **all** the profits. There is **no ceiling** imposed on the financial gains you may enjoy, compared with a lender situation where the interest or return is usually fixed.

Your rights as an owner extend to the full worth of the property, less any loan, including any growth in value of the property that increases your assets. As an owner, if you bought a $100,000 property which subsequently became worth $150,000, the value of your ownership would increase 50%. On the other hand, if you are a lender and lend $25,000 on property valued at $100,000 that subsequently increases in value to $150,000, the value of your loan would remain unchanged.

Property owners usually fare better during inflationary periods than lenders do. Property usually maintains its worth while a dollar loses value, because when the value of your dollars shrinks, it takes more of them to trade for the property.

Other examples of ownership include **part ownership, oil and gas interests, art collectibles and common stock**.

Part-Owner Interest

You may own a part of a business without contributing your services or having a voice in the management, with your risk limited to the amount of your investment. Your ownership interest is not generally transferable; there is no public market for it and it is generally not acceptable as collateral for a loan.

...oil and gas interests... are highly speculative and are typically unsuitable for the average investor.

Oil and Gas Interests

You may invest your capital in ventures such as oil and gas drilling interests. If a well produces oil, you receive a proportionate share of the income earned. These are highly speculative undertakings that are typically unsuitable for the average investor.

Art and Collectibles

Earlier, I mentioned the attributes of attractive investments. In the traditional view of investing, art and collectibles are different from other ownership type investments.

You "manage" your collection and hope to realize profits over time. Originally, the reason for trading your dollars for the collection was in part to enjoy possessing something to wear, such as jewelry, or to decorate your home or office. It takes knowledge and personal involvement to invest intelligently in paintings, sculptures, prints, stamps, coins, photographs and other collectibles. Collecting also requires time – time to be informed, time to enjoy the objects and time for them to appreciate in value. There is, of course, a cost beyond the original investment, since you must pay for insurance against fire and theft and for adequate space to display or store your collection.

Collecting can be a lifetime hobby, but the appreciation in value is best understood by collectors and dealers who are aware of the history and keep up with the collectible market. In trading your dollars for a collectible, consider if you will enjoy possessing the object. Whether it appreciates in value or not will depend on your knowledge of the market and perhaps the artist and on the conditions of the economy at the time of some future trade.

Common Stocks

Common stocks of publicly-owned corporations are an investment that has, to a large degree, the best combination of basic investment attributes. You will find a comparison of these attributes of common stocks with other investment opportunities in Table 14-1.

The ownership of a corporation is indicated by "shares" of what is called common stock. Each share represents a fraction of the total ownership. The term **common** is by no means negative; all owners of a corporation are "common" stockholders.

When you trade dollars for common stocks, you have the most to gain from a successful operation and the most to lose from an unsatisfactory one. Common stocks may come closer to offering all the advantages of an ideal investment than any other medium.

One of the best advantages of "owner" investments is that they are free from the shrinking value of a dollar.

You can blindly accept
what others tell you …

*TIME erodes the value of a dollar but
enhances the value of common stocks.*

If you don't want your money tied to the shrinking value of a dollar, you must develop confidence in the wisdom of investing in common stocks. There are two options available if you want to achieve this. You can either blindly accept what others tell you, or you can take time to study and understand the essential facts that can affect you. Only when you understand the facts can you develop confidence in what you believe and why you believe it.

It is unlikely that you would be reading this book if you intended to rely only on other people for advice. My objective is to try to present, in a simple and straightforward way, the essential facts regarding the characteristics, the short-term risks and the long-term opportunities of owning common stocks.

The history of a long investment record in a group of common stocks was needed to uncover these facts. Probably the best example can be taken from the long-term results of the Dow Jones Industrial Average because it includes a 97-year history of an unmanaged investment in a group of common stocks. The Dow is the oldest and most widely quoted stock market indicator which experts believe represents the overall market at any moment in time. It is made up of a selected group of securities used as an indicator of the performance of all common stocks. Accurate data is available as far back as 1897 and is shown in Chart 13-1.

Occasionally, companies are dropped from the Dow when they are no longer considered representative of the mix of securities in the market and others are added. Even with that adjustment, the Dow still represents the value of a group of securities that is "unmanaged." There are no investment management service or brokerage costs included in the investment results of the Dow.

Initially, the Dow consisted of 12 securities. In 1916 the number was increased to 20. Then in 1928 it was raised to 30, the number still in use.

(13-1) *The Value of the Dow Jones Industrial Average on the First Day of Each Quarter From 1897 Through March 1994* (Dividends **Not** Reinvested)

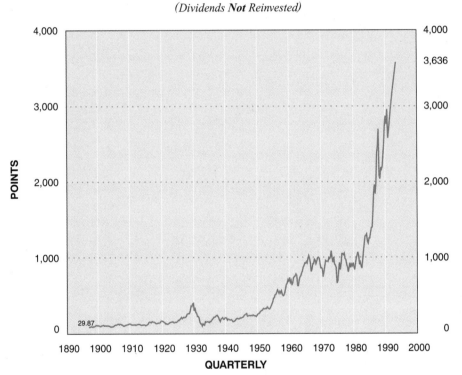

♦ **The Dow's Behavior Over Time**

What should you observe while studying the chart above?

◆ Fluctuations

The value of the Dow fluctuates. Most of the changes are minimal, but occasionally they are dramatic. These major changes, both up and down, are caused mainly by **greed and fear** – emotional reactions to corporate, economic and world news. In good times, people tend to be too optimistic and take the Dow to highs that cannot be supported by reality. In bad times, the tendency is to be too pessimistic (occasionally to the point of panic), which forces the Dow below where it rationally should be.

The value of the Dow fluctuates… occasionally the changes are dramatic.

The Dow moves in cycles, which vary in two ways:
- ◆ Height and depth: Some cycles are much steeper than others.
- ◆ Breadth: Some cycles take much longer to complete than others.

◆ Long-Term Upward Trend

As shown in the chart, the long-term trend of the Dow has been up since 1897. The Dow started at an adjusted value of **29.87** on January 1, 1897. On March 31, 1994, it was **3,636**.

◆ Spurts (uneven trends)

The upward trends are uneven. Many of the major moves are in spurts, few of which were predicted.

◆ Always Rising to New Highs

No matter where you point on the chart, since 1897 the Dow has always risen to new highs over time.

The Opportunity of a Lifetime

Where on the chart of the Dow would you have wanted to make an investment if you could have? Most likely at one of the major lows! However, it would be entirely by luck and accident if you were able to determine the exact lows.

If you can't pick the exact lows, would you rather buy when the Dow is going up or going down? Most people buy when the market is going up, but if you buy when it's going down, you just might earn more money over time. There are two reasons for making more money over time. First, each time you buy when the Dow is falling, you receive more shares for each of your dollars. Second, the value of the Dow has always gone to new highs in time. **Your risk comes only if you are forced to sell your shares at a time when the share price is below your cost.** It takes time for the Dow to go to new highs. Thus, the true risk is not enough TIME. Whenever the price of the Dow is at or near a major low, it probably presents you with a great opportunity.

Most people buy when the market is going up, but if you buy when it's going down, you just might earn more money over time.

◆ Value of the Dow Versus a Dollar Over Time

Although one cannot invest directly in the Dow, the following study relates to an assumed investment in the Dow. The next chart shows the value of $1 invested in the Dow with all dividends reinvested from 1897 through 1993. This illustrates the total return of the Dow Jones Industrial Average. Also on this chart is the value of a 1900 dollar over time.

Chart 13-2 indicates that one 1900 dollar ($1.00) kept in a **safe** place could be traded for approximately six cents' ($0.06) worth of goods or services at the end of 1993. On the other hand, if the same dollar had been invested in the unmanaged Dow, it could have been exchanged in 1993 for 11,220 dollars.

The line representing the value of $1 invested in the Dow on January 1, 1897, appears to be close to zero until a little after 1940. This is not as it appears. The actual values at the end of various periods of time are shown in Chart 13-3.

(13-2)

The Value of $1 Invested in the Dow From 1897 Through 1993, Compared to the Diminishing Value of a 1900 Dollar

*(With **All** Dividends Reinvested and Compounded)*

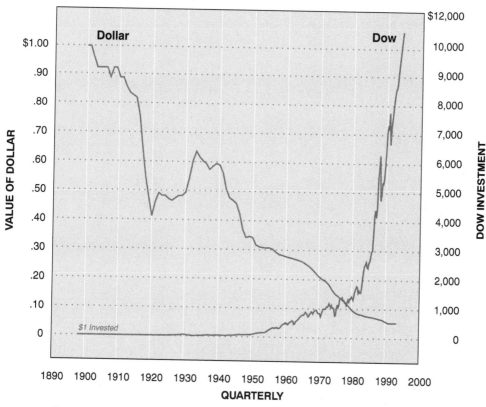

Source: Data provided by Bureau of the Census and Bureau of Labor Statistics.

Chart 13-3, on the next page, shows that if you multiply the last figure by 10,000, you will determine that $10,000 invested in the Dow on January 1, 1897, with all dividends reinvested and no consideration given for taxes, would have been worth $112,208,600 at the end of 1993, a 97-year period. The annual average percent return over that period was 10.08%.

(13-3)   *Actual Value of $1 Invested in the Dow on January 1, 1897*
(With All Dividends Reinvested)

YEAR	VALUE AT END OF YEAR
1897	$ 1.25
1900	1.98
1920	7.25
1940	35.90
1960	466.50
1980	1,682.86
1990	7,193.81
1991	8,933.83
1992	9,595.63
1993	11,220.86

Note that as the 1900 dollar lost value over time, the Dow, with all dividends reinvested, rose dramatically above the rate of the reduced worth of the dollar. The rise more than compensated for the loss in value of the 1900 dollar.

...the value of the Dow has always returned to the point where it had been...

Except for a brief period between 1920-1932, the value of the dollar has steadily declined. In contrast, when the Dow falls, the value of the Dow has always returned to the point where it had been and continued to rise above it later. However, both the shrinking dollar value and gain in the Dow Jones Industrial Average did take TIME.

◆ Value of the Dow Adjusted for Dollar Loss

The next chart demonstrates the results of trading $1 for units of the Dow on January 1, 1897, and adjusting the value of those units for the declining value of a 1900 dollar over a 97-year period. These results include all reinvested dividends.

(13-4)   *Adjusted Value of $1 Invested in the Dow From 1897 Through 1993*
*(With **All** Dividends Reinvested)*

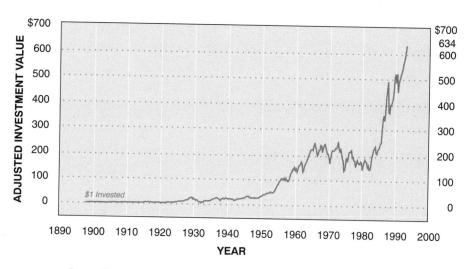

Source: Data provided by Bureau of the Census and Bureau of Labor Statistics.

A 1900 dollar invested in the Dow was worth $11,220 on December 31, 1993. If this result is adjusted for the loss in value, the chart above shows that the adjusted value would be $634, which is 634 times greater than a 1900 dollar. Obviously the increase in value of this hypothetical investment in the Dow more than compensated for the loss in value of a dollar.

This chart highlights the importance of trading a dollar for something that can maintain or exceed its original value.

TIME erodes the value of a dollar
but enhances the value of common stocks.

There are short-term risks and long-term opportunities…

Where Will the Dow Be in 10 Years?

No one can predict the future, but if a dollar were to lose one-half of its value in the next 10 years, the value of the Dow would have to double just to keep up with the loss in value of a dollar. If this happened, the Dow Jones Industrial Average would have to increase from 3,754 to over 7,508 by the end of the year 2003.

If you ever think that the value of the Dow may be too high, take time and ask yourself: Do you consider it **too high today**, when compared with where it has been in the past, or do you consider it too high when compared with where the Dow might be **in the future?**

Why do Financial Markets React the Way They Do?

To understand the actions of financial markets, it is first necessary to learn about the actions of a large number of people that make up that market. Years ago, it was suggested that I read the book "The Crowd," written in 1841 by a Frenchman named LeBon. I will never forget what I learned from reading that book. The author studied the reactions of crowds. He came to the conclusion that **the intelligence of a crowd is lower than the intelligence of the individuals that make up the crowd.** It is my belief that people buying and selling securities in the market are a crowd and they behave like a crowd. If this is correct, **the intelligence of the "market crowd" is less rational than the intelligence of the individual people in the market.** It is very important to keep this fact in mind.

While trying to understand the reactions of financial markets, **focus your attention on the market itself rather than on the individual securities that make up that market.**

It is normal for the value of the stock market to go up and down. The market has done this for years and will continue to do so. It is also normal that greed at times causes investors to push the value of stocks in the market to levels far beyond what a rational investor would be willing to pay. Eventually, **if the market is not going to go further up, it will come down.** When the market falls, it is also normal that **fear** causes the "market crowd" to sell stock. Extreme "fear selling" causes the market to fall far below its realistic value. In time, when stocks eventually get into firmer hands and investors become convinced the market has reached the bottom, the market will turn around. **If the market is not going to go down any further, it will certainly go up.**

It is *not* **normal for the market to continue to advance upward and never stop.** Why? The value of all securities will never go in the same direction at the same time. If they did, this would create an extremely emotional crisis, and this would make the "market crowd" feel extremely uncomfortable. Is the market getting too high? To satisfy this emotional condition, the market must come down and then prove to the "market crowd" that it can advance back later through its previous high. If the market does advance above the previous high, it gives the "market crowd" confidence that it can go higher.

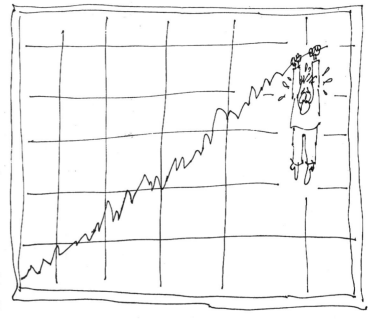

Enthusiasm and greed maintain this process of "testing for the high" until the time comes when the market will not break out to a new high. A large percentage of the "market crowd" will have to believe that the market will not advance further. When it becomes convinced the market is too high, it is not going to advance further. **If the market is not going to go up any further, it is certainly going to go down.**

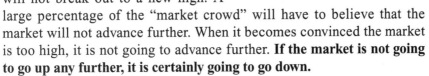

Is the market getting too high?

It is normal for the market to fall. When this occurs, the process described above is reversed. The "market crowd" will sell securities thus lowering the value of the market. How far the market falls depends on the emotion of the "market crowd." The market will fall until **it does not fall below the previous low.** It will fall until stocks eventually get into firmer hands and investors become convinced the market has reached the bottom. Then, and only then, will the market turn around. **If the market is not going to go down any further, it will certainly go up.**

Market Reactions Are Normal.
        Expect Reactions to Reoccur in the Future.

If market reactions are normal, why panic because of a sudden sharp drop in the stock market if you believe the value of the Dow Jones Industrial Average can double in the next 10 years.

The greatest long-term financial risk you face is **not** stock market reactions. The market, in time, has always bounced back from lows and has always gone on to new highs. **Your greatest long-term financial risk is the continual loss in the value of a dollar.** For example, one (1) 1900 dollar is worth less than 6 cents today. It has lost over 94% of its value.

If a dollar loses 6.7% of its value each year for 10 years, that dollar would lose one-half its value and would be worth only 50 cents. It is hoped this does not happen, but it could. If it does happen, then the value of the Dow Jones Industrial Average would have to at least double in order to compensate for that loss in value of a dollar. The Dow Jones has compensated for the loss in value of a dollar in the past.

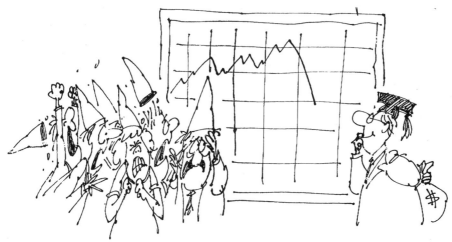

The (combined) intelligence of the stock market crowd is less rational than the individual investor.

Financial Markets React the Way They Do Because:

♦ **The intelligence of the "market crowd" is less rational than the intelligence of the individuals in the market.**

♦ **It is normal for the market to go up and down.**

♦ It is normal that greed at times causes the "market crowd" to push the value of stocks in the market up to levels far beyond what a rational investor would be willing to pay. **If the market is not going to go up any further, it is certainly going down.**

♦ It is normal that fear and panic at times cause the market to fall far below its realistic value. **If the market is not going to go down any further, it will certainly go up.**

♦ The greatest long-term financial risk anyone faces is **not** stock market reactions. The market, in time, has always bounced back and has always gone on to new highs. **The greatest long-term financial risk everyone faces is the continual loss in the value of a dollar.**

Assumed Investments in the Dow

What are the short-term investment risks and the long-term investment opportunities of owning common stocks? To get a historical point of view, detailed studies were made of assumed investments in an unmanaged group of common stocks represented by the Dow Jones Industrial Average. This study covered various investment periods during the 97-year history of the Dow.

The purpose of this analysis was to identify the best and worst investment results for each selected period and to determine when these results occurred. Another objective was to identify where the middle 50% of the investment results occurred for each period.

Case I of this study assumes a **one-time investment of $10,000.**

Case II assumes **$100 is invested each month.**

In both cases, all dividends are reinvested.

The following assumptions were also made for both cases:

They included 97.25 years beginning January 1897, and ending March 31, 1994.

The money was invested in multiple "rolling" periods: one, three, five, 10, 15, 20, 25, and 30 years.

The starting point of the first investment period began on the first day of 1897 and lasted the duration of one of the multiple periods (one, three, five, 10, 15, 20, 25, and 30 years). The next investment period started at the beginning of the second quarter (April 1897) and also lasted the duration of one of the multiple periods. This process continued to advance one quarter of a year at a time until the last investment period ended on March 31, 1994.

There were 386 one-year investment periods during 97 years. Chart 13-5 illustrates how the one-year investment periods relate to each other.

The results of both cases demonstrate how an investment in the Dow fluctuates over various periods of time. They clearly illustrate the short-term risks and the long-term opportunities of such investments.

(13-5)   *One-Year Investment Periods*
                                Each Starting at the Beginning of a Quarter

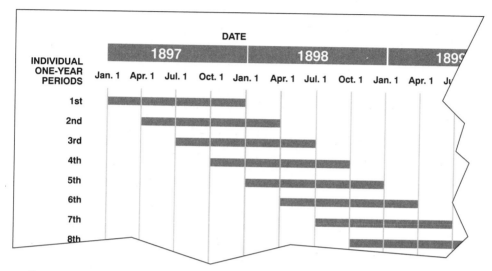

♦ **Case I – One-Time Investment of $10,000**

    Case I follows an investment of $10,000 traded for units of the Dow.
Remember, as long as it was held in those units, the investment was not
tied to a dollar but instead was tied to the value of the Dow. At the beginning of each period considered, it was assumed a **one-time investment**
was made on the first business day of that quarter. All dividends were
reinvested immediately in additional units.

    At the end of each individual period, the accumulated units of the Dow
were traded back into dollars. Thus, each investment started with $10,000
and ended with a new dollar value. The difference between the starting
and ending figures was converted to an **average annual percentage
return**. The individual percentage returns were then listed in order, from
the highest returns to the lowest.

Understanding the Case Study Charts

The easiest way to visualize and comprehend this information is through the use of simple charts. It is important that you take time to examine the individual elements in the charts. Try to understand and become comfortable with how **they were developed.*** This will help you interpret the results of the study.

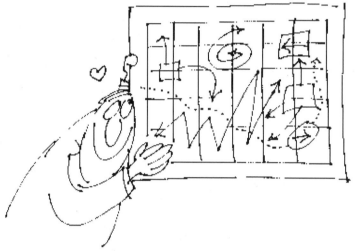

Try to understand and become comfortable with the charts.

The elements are built up in Charts 13-6A through 13-6C to arrive at the final chart, 13-6D.

(13-6A)

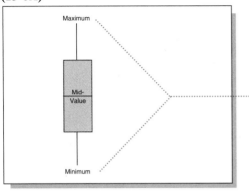

Range of all investment results for the total number of individual periods covered with best results on the top and the worst at the bottom

(13-6B)

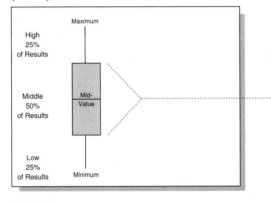

50% of the investment results are contained in this box

25% fall above the Mid-Value and 25% fall below

(13-6C)

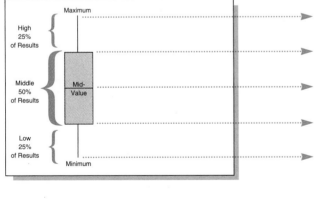

Best investment result for the individual period

Top of the Middle 50% of Results

Value of the midpoint of all investment results for this period

Bottom of the Middle 50% of Results

Worst investment result for the individual period

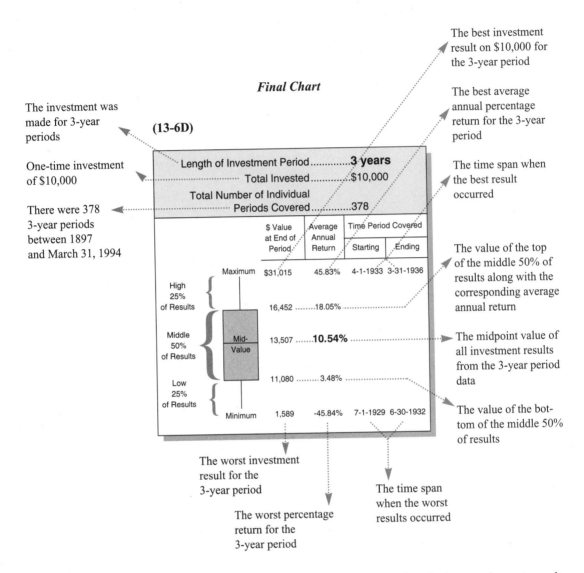

Final Chart

(13-6D)

The investment was made for 3-year periods

One-time investment of $10,000

There were 378 3-year periods between 1897 and March 31, 1994

Length of Investment Period .... **3 years**
Total Invested $10,000
Total Number of Individual Periods Covered 378

The best investment result on $10,000 for the 3-year period

The best average annual percentage return for the 3-year period

The time span when the best result occurred

The value of the top of the middle 50% of results along with the corresponding average annual return

The midpoint value of all investment results from the 3-year period data

The value of the bottom of the middle 50% of results

	$ Value at End of Period	Average Annual Return	Time Period Covered	
			Starting	Ending
Maximum	$31,015	45.83%	4-1-1933	3-31-1936
High 25% of Results	16,452	18.05%		
Middle 50% of Results — Mid-Value	13,507	**10.54%**		
Low 25% of Results	11,080	3.48%		
Minimum	1,589	-45.84%	7-1-1929	6-30-1932

The worst investment result for the 3-year period

The worst percentage return for the 3-year period

The time span when the worst results occurred

You may be as curious as I was to learn what the best and worst results were in each period and when they occurred. The following charts indicate the results for individual periods of time. Please note that these charts are **not** drawn to scale. Charts 13-7A and 13-7B summarize all of the eight individual periods (one, three, five, 10, 15, 20, 25, and 30 years).

(13-7A)

Amount of Investment. . . . . $10,000 One Time
Investment in. . . . . Dow Jones Industrial Average
(With All Distributions Reinvested)
Time Period Covered. . . . . 1897 through March 1994
(Progressing one quarter at a time)

Length of Investment Period..............**1 year**
Total Invested..............$10,000
Total Number of Individual
Periods Covered..............386

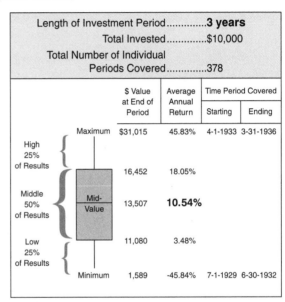

		$ Value at End of Period	Annual Return	Time Period Covered Starting	Time Period Covered Ending
	Maximum	$23,813	138.13%	7-1-1932	6-30-1933
High 25% of Results		12,671	26.71%		
Middle 50% of Results	Mid-Value	11,059	**10.59%**		
Low 25% of Results		9,667	-3.33%		
	Minimum	3,109	-68.91%	7-1-1931	6-30-1932

Length of Investment Period..............**3 years**
Total Invested..............$10,000
Total Number of Individual
Periods Covered..............378

		$ Value at End of Period	Average Annual Return	Time Period Covered Starting	Time Period Covered Ending
	Maximum	$31,015	45.83%	4-1-1933	3-31-1936
High 25% of Results		16,452	18.05%		
Middle 50% of Results	Mid-Value	13,507	**10.54%**		
Low 25% of Results		11,080	3.48%		
	Minimum	1,589	-45.84%	7-1-1929	6-30-1932

Length of Investment Period..............**5 years**
Total Invested..............$10,000
Total Number of Individual
Periods Covered..............370

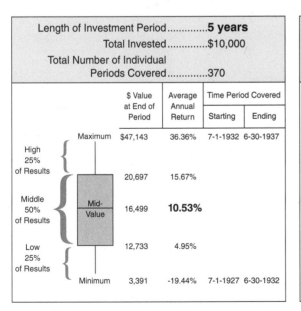

		$ Value at End of Period	Average Annual Return	Time Period Covered Starting	Time Period Covered Ending
	Maximum	$47,143	36.36%	7-1-1932	6-30-1937
High 25% of Results		20,697	15.67%		
Middle 50% of Results	Mid-Value	16,499	**10.53%**		
Low 25% of Results		12,733	4.95%		
	Minimum	3,391	-19.44%	7-1-1927	6-30-1932

Length of Investment Period..............**10 years**
Total Invested..............$10,000
Total Number of Individual
Periods Covered..............350

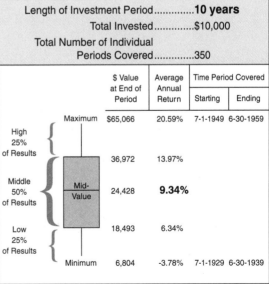

		$ Value at End of Period	Average Annual Return	Time Period Covered Starting	Time Period Covered Ending
	Maximum	$65,066	20.59%	7-1-1949	6-30-1959
High 25% of Results		36,972	13.97%		
Middle 50% of Results	Mid-Value	24,428	**9.34%**		
Low 25% of Results		18,493	6.34%		
	Minimum	6,804	-3.78%	7-1-1929	6-30-1939

Not Drawn to Scale.

(13-7B)

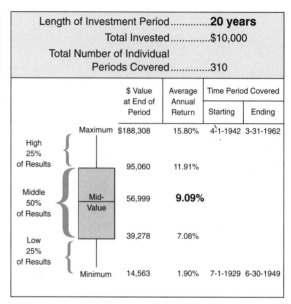

Length of Investment Period..............**15 years**				
Total Invested..............$10,000				
Total Number of Individual Periods Covered..............330				

| | $ Value at End of Period | Average Annual Return | Time Period Covered | |
			Starting	Ending
Maximum	$140,726	19.63%	10-1-1914	9-30-1929
High 25% of Results	60,509	12.75%		
Middle 50% of Results (Mid-Value)	38,041	**9.31%**		
	25,792	6.52%		
Low 25% of Results				
Minimum	9,849	-0.10%	10-1-1929	9-30-1944

Length of Investment Period..............**20 years**				
Total Invested..............$10,000				
Total Number of Individual Periods Covered..............310				

| | $ Value at End of Period | Average Annual Return | Time Period Covered | |
			Starting	Ending
Maximum	$188,308	15.80%	4-1-1942	3-31-1962
High 25% of Results	95,060	11.91%		
Middle 50% of Results (Mid-Value)	56,999	**9.09%**		
	39,278	7.08%		
Low 25% of Results				
Minimum	14,563	1.90%	7-1-1929	6-30-1949

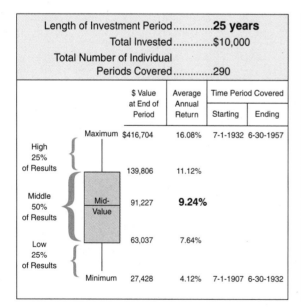

Length of Investment Period..............**25 years**				
Total Invested..............$10,000				
Total Number of Individual Periods Covered..............290				

| | $ Value at End of Period | Average Annual Return | Time Period Covered | |
			Starting	Ending
Maximum	$416,704	16.08%	7-1-1932	6-30-1957
High 25% of Results	139,806	11.12%		
Middle 50% of Results (Mid-Value)	91,227	**9.24%**		
	63,037	7.64%		
Low 25% of Results				
Minimum	27,428	4.12%	7-1-1907	6-30-1932

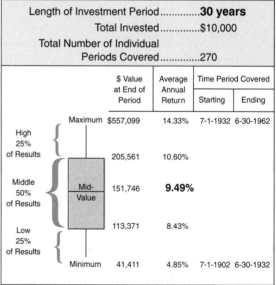

Length of Investment Period..............**30 years**				
Total Invested..............$10,000				
Total Number of Individual Periods Covered..............270				

| | $ Value at End of Period | Average Annual Return | Time Period Covered | |
			Starting	Ending
Maximum	$557,099	14.33%	7-1-1932	6-30-1962
High 25% of Results	205,561	10.60%		
Middle 50% of Results (Mid-Value)	151,746	**9.49%**		
	113,371	8.43%		
Low 25% of Results				
Minimum	41,411	4.85%	7-1-1902	6-30-1932

Not Drawn to Scale.

Compare the one-time $10,000 investment with the "$ Value at End of Period." See how these values change with the length of investment period.

Look at the **one-year** chart 13-7A. There was a wide variance in annual return results, with a total spread of over 207%, from 138% for the best one-year period to a minus 69% for the worst. It is interesting to note that the best one-year period was from July 1, 1932, to June 30, 1933, while the worst one-year period began one year earlier, July 1, 1931, and ended when the best results started, June 30, 1932.

An investment made on July 1, 1931, would have realized, one year later, the worst one-year result out of 386 periods (minus 69%). Most people, if they had experienced these poor results, would have assumed that this was an indication of future performance and would have become discouraged. Many would have traded their investment back for dollars and tried to find another place to invest their money. Had they had confidence in the long-term opportunities in the Dow and left their investment undisturbed for another 29 years (30 years total), it would have been worth $211,359. The original investment, which began with the worst one-year result, **grew at an average annual compound rate of 10.7%** (one of the best 30-year results). As you can see, **it is unwise to assume that short-term investment results are an accurate indication of long-term performance.**

In the other charts, observe the best and worst "$ Value at End of Period." In each of the charts, pay special attention to the results of the **Middle 50% of Results.**

Observe that, in five out of the eight investment periods, the lowest result ended on June 30, 1932. Also notice that, in four of the eight periods, the best results started at the quarter beginning on July 1, 1932.

(13-8) *$10,000 Investments in the Dow Jones Industrial Average*

(With All Dividends Reinvested)

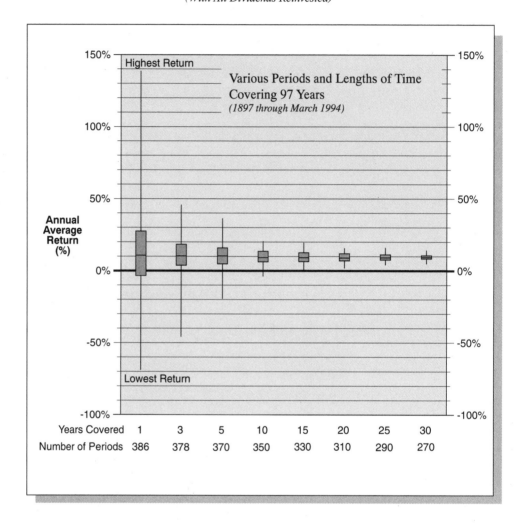

The chart above is drawn to scale. It presents the data from the preceding charts for comparative purposes. Beginning with the one-year period, the difference between the highest percentage return and the lowest return narrowed more rapidly the longer the investment was held. The spread in returns for the one-year period was 207%. This spread decreased for the 30-year period to only 9%. The 30-year results ranged from a high of 14% to a low of 5%, with the majority of results between 11% and 8%.

What, then, is the message? The longer an investment was held in the Dow, the less risk there was of suffering a loss. Starting with the 20-year period, there were **no losses at all**! Moreover, for each of the **Middle 50% of Results**, there were no losses starting with the three-year periods.

The table below illustrates the results of the study in a different way. This approach may appeal to those who think dealing in the stock market is like gambling, because it shows the probability of receiving a certain percentage return. It indicates the percentage of results which were in excess of various compound rates. It also indicates the total number of results within each period.

(13-9)   ***The Probability of Receiving a Certain Return***
$10,000 Investments in the Dow Jones Industrial Average
(With All Dividends Reinvested)

Comparing Various Periods and Percentage Rates

Covering 97 Years (1897 through March 1994)
*Percentage Results **in Excess of** Various Compound Rates*

PERIOD (YEARS)	0%	2%	4%	6%	8%	10%	12%	14%	16%	18%	20%	22%	24%	26%	28%	30%	NUMBER OF PERIODS
1	70	67	63	60	55	51	47	44	41	38	34	32	29	25	23	20	386
3	88	80	73	65	58	53	42	37	31	25	20	14	9	6	4	2	378
5	90	86	78	69	61	52	41	32	23	15	11	6	3	2	2	1	370
10	97	95	89	77	62	44	33	24	13	4	0	0	0	0	0	0	350
15	99	97	92	78	64	43	30	17	5	0	0	0	0	0	0	0	330
20	100	99	97	88	64	44	25	5	0	0	0	0	0	0	0	0	310
25	100	100	100	97	68	38	16	2	0	0	0	0	0	0	0	0	290
30	100	100	100	99	85	34	8	0	0	0	0	0	0	0	0	0	270

▲*

* There was only one 97.25 year investment period which had an average annual return of 10.01%.

What was the probability of making money if you invested in the Dow for only one year? The chart indicates that there was a 70% chance of having a positive return. **The opportunity for a positive return increased the longer the investment was held**. After 20 years, the chart indicates there was a 100% probability of earning a positive return.

Focus on the 6% column. Notice that the probability of receiving more than a 6% return increased from 60% for the one-year period to 99% for the 30-year period.

Look at the probability of receiving more than 14% over time. The probability rapidly **decreased** from 44% for the one-year period to 0% for the 30-year period.

If you are interested in learning what percentage of the 10-year period results received between an 8% and a 10% return, locate the probability percentages on the 10-year period line under the 8% and 10% columns and subtract one percentage figure from the other. For example in Table 13-9, if you subtract 44 from 62, you will find that 18% of the 10-year period results received an average of between 8% and 10%.

Overall, notice in Table 13-9 how the long-term probability results tend to "funnel" toward a 10% return in the 30-year period.

◆ Case II – An Investment of $100 a Month

You have seen the results of a one-time $10,000 investment. Since this amount might seem beyond your reach, it might be easier for you to relate to a $100-a-month investment. If this is the case, you might be curious to learn what were the best and worst results over various periods of time and when they occurred. Also, you might be interested in learning what the probabilities were of receiving a certain return and what was the effect of time on this regular investment.

Case II follows an investment of $100 a month with all dividends reinvested. The same assumptions of Case I could refer also to this segment.

While there is much that one can learn from these charts, let me highlight two key observations.

In the following $100-a-month investment charts:

1. **Every one** of the lowest results happened to end on the same date: June 30, 1932.

(13-10A)

Amount of Investment.........$100 a Month
Investment in.........Dow Jones Industrial Average
(With All Distributions Reinvested)
Time Period Covered.........1897 through March 1994
(Progressing one quarter at a time)

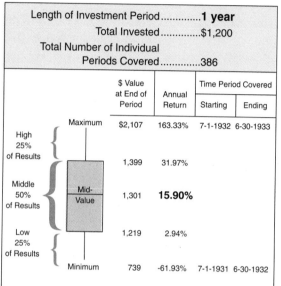

| Length of Investment Period.............**1 year** |
| Total Invested.............$1,200 |
| Total Number of Individual Periods Covered.............386 |

	$ Value at End of Period	Annual Return	Time Period Covered	
			Starting	Ending
Maximum	$2,107	163.33%	7-1-1932	6-30-1933
High 25% of Results	1,399	31.97%		
Middle 50% of Results — Mid-Value	1,301	**15.90%**		
Low 25% of Results	1,219	2.94%		
Minimum	739	-61.93%	7-1-1931	6-30-1932

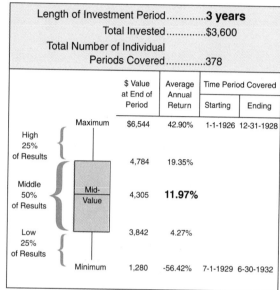

| Length of Investment Period.............**3 years** |
| Total Invested.............$3,600 |
| Total Number of Individual Periods Covered.............378 |

	$ Value at End of Period	Average Annual Return	Time Period Covered	
			Starting	Ending
Maximum	$6,544	42.90%	1-1-1926	12-31-1928
High 25% of Results	4,784	19.35%		
Middle 50% of Results — Mid-Value	4,305	**11.97%**		
Low 25% of Results	3,842	4.27%		
Minimum	1,280	-56.42%	7-1-1929	6-30-1932

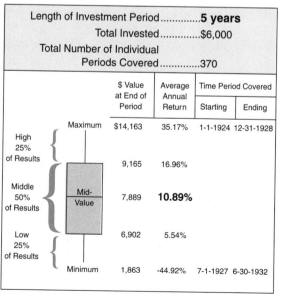

| Length of Investment Period.............**5 years** |
| Total Invested.............$6,000 |
| Total Number of Individual Periods Covered.............370 |

	$ Value at End of Period	Average Annual Return	Time Period Covered	
			Starting	Ending
Maximum	$14,163	35.17%	1-1-1924	12-31-1928
High 25% of Results	9,165	16.96%		
Middle 50% of Results — Mid-Value	7,889	**10.89%**		
Low 25% of Results	6,902	5.54%		
Minimum	1,863	-44.92%	7-1-1927	6-30-1932

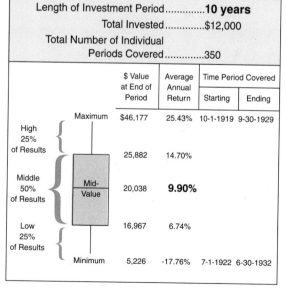

| Length of Investment Period.............**10 years** |
| Total Invested.............$12,000 |
| Total Number of Individual Periods Covered.............350 |

	$ Value at End of Period	Average Annual Return	Time Period Covered	
			Starting	Ending
Maximum	$46,177	25.43%	10-1-1919	9-30-1929
High 25% of Results	25,882	14.70%		
Middle 50% of Results — Mid-Value	20,038	**9.90%**		
Low 25% of Results	16,967	6.74%		
Minimum	5,226	-17.76%	7-1-1922	6-30-1932

Not Drawn to Scale.

(13-10B)

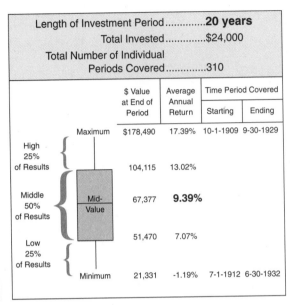

		$ Value at End of Period	Average Annual Return	Time Period Covered	
				Starting	Ending
	Maximum	$95,165	19.95%	7-1-1914	6-30-1929
High 25% of Results		55,920	13.88%		
Middle 50% of Results	Mid-Value	39,443	**9.79%**		
		30,262	6.59%		
Low 25% of Results					
	Minimum	11,252	-6.57%	7-1-1917	6-30-1932

Length of Investment Period ....**15 years**
Total Invested $18,000
Total Number of Individual Periods Covered 330

Length of Investment Period ....**20 years**
Total Invested $24,000
Total Number of Individual Periods Covered 310

		$ Value at End of Period	Average Annual Return	Time Period Covered	
				Starting	Ending
	Maximum	$178,490	17.39%	10-1-1909	9-30-1929
High 25% of Results		104,115	13.02%		
Middle 50% of Results	Mid-Value	67,377	**9.39%**		
		51,470	7.07%		
Low 25% of Results					
	Minimum	21,331	-1.19%	7-1-1912	6-30-1932

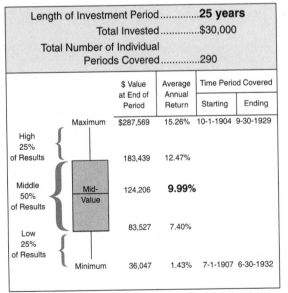

Length of Investment Period ....**25 years**
Total Invested $30,000
Total Number of Individual Periods Covered 290

		$ Value at End of Period	Average Annual Return	Time Period Covered	
				Starting	Ending
	Maximum	$287,569	15.26%	10-1-1904	9-30-1929
High 25% of Results		183,439	12.47%		
Middle 50% of Results	Mid-Value	124,206	**9.99%**		
		83,527	7.40%		
Low 25% of Results					
	Minimum	36,047	1.43%	7-1-1907	6-30-1932

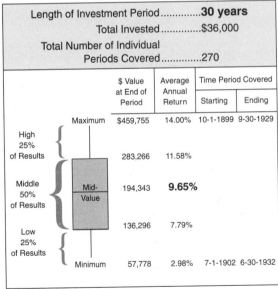

Length of Investment Period ....**30 years**
Total Invested $36,000
Total Number of Individual Periods Covered 270

		$ Value at End of Period	Average Annual Return	Time Period Covered	
				Starting	Ending
	Maximum	$459,755	14.00%	10-1-1899	9-30-1929
High 25% of Results		283,266	11.58%		
Middle 50% of Results	Mid-Value	194,343	**9.65%**		
		136,296	7.79%		
Low 25% of Results					
	Minimum	57,778	2.98%	7-1-1902	6-30-1932

Not Drawn to Scale.

2. If each of these eight investments had been held just one more year, with no further investment and not traded back into dollars, they would have all gained 138% or increased 2.38 times, because the best "one-year" investment period result began on the next day, July 1, 1932 (see one-year investment period in Chart 13-7A).

(13-11) *$100 a Month Invested in the Dow Jones Industrial Average*

(With All Dividends Reinvested)

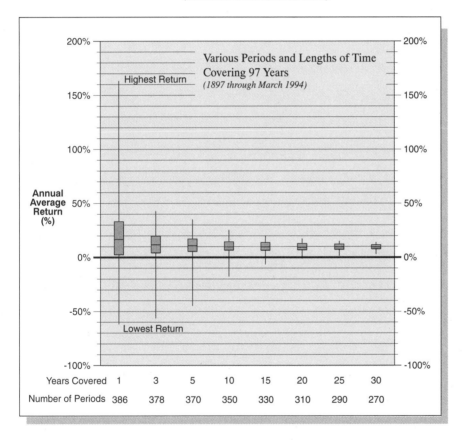

The data from the preceding charts is drawn to scale for comparative purposes in Chart 13-11. You can also compare the differences and similarities to the $10,000 charts in Chart 13-8.

(13-12)   *The Probability of Receiving a Certain Return*
                          $100-a-Month Investments in the Dow Jones Industrial Average
                                         (With All Dividends Reinvested)
                              Comparing Various Periods and Percentage Rates
                               Covering 97 Years (1897 through March 1994)
                            *Percentage Results **in Excess of** Various Compound Rates*

PERIOD (YEARS)	0%	2%	4%	6%	8%	10%	12%	14%	16%	18%	20%	22%	24%	26%	28%	30%	NUMBER OF PERIODS
1	78	76	73	70	67	63	59	54	50	47	42	39	35	32	30	27	386
3	85	81	76	67	62	55	49	42	36	29	23	20	15	12	10	7	378
5	90	86	80	73	63	55	44	33	27	22	16	10	7	5	2	2	370
10	96	94	90	78	64	49	37	28	17	10	4	1	1	0	0	0	350
15	99	97	93	79	64	47	36	24	13	1	0	0	0	0	0	0	330
20	99	99	97	85	65	47	34	18	1	0	0	0	0	0	0	0	310
25	100	99	99	92	66	49	28	7	0	0	0	0	0	0	0	0	290
30	100	100	99	98	70	44	19	0	0	0	0	0	0	0	0	0	270

The table above shows the probability of receiving a certain rate of return while investing $100 a month. Compare these probabilities with those of a $10,000 investment shown in Table 13-9. If you study the similar periods and percentage rates of these charts, you will see that **the probability of receiving a higher percentage rate over time is generally slightly greater with periodic investments, in this case $100 a month**.

Summary

Here are some of the conclusions you can draw from these case studies of the Dow. **Even though there was no professional investment management, the long-term gains were impressive.**

There **were** short-term risks.

It is unwise to assume that short-term investment results are always a true indication of long-term performance.

There were long-term opportunities available if the investment was left alone.

Many people believe that investing is a form of gambling. In a way, this may appear to be true in the short term. The probabilities for profit on the investment significantly increased by lengthening the time the investment was held.

The importance of TIME cannot be overemphasized.

No one knows what will actually happen in the future, but the past **is** certainly an indication of what could happen.

Some questions to ask yourself:

If you had traded your money for an investment in the Dow and left it undisturbed for years, would you have been satisfied with the long-term results?

Is an investment kept in the Dow for more than three years not as much of a gamble as you once thought?

Do you believe this investment in common stocks keeps pace with and stays ahead of the loss in value of a dollar?

Do you believe this is a safe place to put your money over time?

Do you believe you would feel comfortable investing in the Dow over a long period of time?

Do you realize the probability of receiving a higher percentage rate is generally a little greater with a $100 a month than with a one-time investment?

Do you think you could expect better results having professionals manage your money?

There are short-term risks.

The purpose of an investment company
is to manage money professionally.

Managed Investments – Investment Companies

*I have never owned any marketable equity securities
other than shares of mutual funds.*

In 1924, bankers in New England introduced the investment company concept to America. For many years, these companies were not generally accepted by the investing public because of abuses in their operations and the absence of effective regulations. However, the Investment Company Act of 1940 provided safety measures which helped erase doubts about this type of investment.

After World War II, the full potential of the investment company concept began to be realized. This was due not only to restored public confidence, but also to a long rising market trend and the growing interest of people who had dollars to invest.

The purpose of an investment company is to manage money professionally. It provides a place where investors can pool their money, employ full-time professionals and pursue the goal of earning money with their money. The investment company belongs to the shareholders, not to management. It provides all the advantages usually available only to large investors.

Types of Investment Companies

There are two basic types of investment companies, **closed-end** and **open-end**. A closed-end company sells its shares to you but does not agree to buy back those shares in the future. If you buy shares of a closed-end investment company and want to sell them, you must find a buyer either in the over-the-counter market or on the stock exchange if the shares are traded there. Shares of closed-end investment companies often trade at a price below their asset value.

An open-end investment company is usually called a **mutual fund**. It not only sells shares to you but **also agrees to buy the shares back** at whatever their value might be in the future.

Investment companies are further categorized as **diversified** and **non-diversified**. With respect to 75% of the total value of the assets, a diversified company may invest no more than 5% in the securities of any one company or acquire more than 10% of the outstanding voting securities of a company. In addition, the typical diversified fund also follows a policy which prohibits the investment of more than 25% of its assets in any one industry. These requirements force diversification among various investments.

A non-diversified company is simply one that is not diversified. Of the two, the diversified investment company is the more popular.

All investment companies charge for professional management and shareholder services.

The **most** popular open-end companies, **mutual funds**, are further categorized as **load funds** or **no-load funds**.

Load Versus No-Load Funds

Load funds have a **sales charge** when you buy shares or when you sell (deferred sales charges) or both. These funds are usually distributed through brokers. These sales charges are over and above the investment management and shareholder servicing costs. Sales charges are used to pay commissions to brokers.

No-load funds **have no sales charge**, although there are still investment management and shareholder servicing costs which are paid for by the mutual fund itself.

Some funds, load or no-load, also have an annual charge for marketing expenses (12b-1 charges) shared by all fund shareholders because the fund pays these expenses directly.

Investment Objectives

Each mutual fund has a specific investment objective with clearly stated investment policies and restrictions. Some are imposed by the founders of the fund and some are imposed by law. Changes in a fund's investment objective or those investment policies or restrictions which are considered fundamental must be approved by its shareholders.

The investment objectives, restrictions, policies and all costs of a fund are described in great detail in a fact book called a **prospectus**, which is required to be made available by all funds. This document should be read carefully before purchasing fund shares to ensure that a fund's investment objectives coincide with yours.

◆ Policies that Differentiate Mutual Funds

Funds with the fewest restrictions allow the investment managers broad authority to use their best judgment to determine:

What to invest in.

Where to invest.

How much to invest.

How long to invest.

How much cash to hold if attractive investments cannot be found.

I would describe a fund that gives this broad authority to an investment manager as a **fully-managed fund**, since minimal limitations are

A shareholder ... can relax and rely on the best judgment of the fund manager.

placed on management. Because of this broad authority, a shareholder having confidence in such a fund can relax and rely on the best judgment of the fund manager.

Funds with more restrictive policies **limit the investment manager** in the exercise of his best judgment when choosing investments that best match the fund's objective. For example, if a fund is prohibited from making investments in certain industries or is restricted to investing in one geographic area, the investment manager's best judgment is limited. In this case, the shareholder must be constantly alert and continue to make decisions about when to invest and when to redeem.

Some Attributes of Mutual Funds

I mentioned earlier the attributes of "ideal" investments. Now, let's relate these to mutual funds.

◆ Professional Management

Professional money management has long been available to large institutions and wealthy investors. Mutual funds make this kind of financial expertise available to everyone.

Mutual funds make professional money management available to everyone.

I believe that **professional management is the most important contribution to investment success over time**. The qualities of professional

management described here are taken from my personal experience over the past 34 years since founding Twentieth Century Mutual Funds.

First and foremost, mutual fund managers are full-time professionals dedicated to managing the money invested in their funds. They bring to this trusted responsibility a specialized team of researchers, analysts, and state-of-the-art technology to ensure that the money invested, no matter what the amount, is given full-time attention. They invest, reinvest and seek the best opportunities for the assets they manage.

Admittedly, professional managers are not infallible. They may err in judgment and losses may occur on their selections. But usually **full-time, thoroughly trained managers and their support systems can do a better job than most individuals. Also, the results of their effort can be judged by their performance over time**.

◆ Diversification

Spreading investments over a number of different companies is advantageous, since some companies may lose value while others prosper. Mutual funds offer **instant diversification** on any amount of money. One share of a mutual fund represents part-ownership in a portfolio that holds many companies. Furthermore, diversification spreads risk not only over many companies, but also over many industries. Before mutual funds, diversification was a privilege largely available only to the wealthy who could diversify and purchase many securities.

Before mutual funds, diversification was a privilege largely available only to the wealthy who could diversify and purchase many securities.

For a mutual fund
investor, liquidity is
very important.

◆ Liquidity

For a mutual fund investor, liquidity is very important. Open-end mutual funds agree to redeem their shares each market day at their closing prices, usually called "net asset value." Shareholders can withdraw part or all of their investment at any time.

◆ Opportunity for Growth

Many investments are made with the hope of gain or growth. While there is no guarantee, judging by the past, common stock mutual funds certainly offer an opportunity for capital growth, particularly over the long term.

◆ Record Keeping

An important feature of mutual funds is that they are able to provide a complete record of your transactions.

When you own a share of a mutual fund, you are not required to keep records of the holdings represented by your ownership interest. The mutual fund company does it for you. If you owned shares of all the companies owned by the fund, you would have to keep individual records for each company, which would certainly be a burdensome job.

◆ Availability in Convenient Amounts

Many investment options require a large initial investment, which closes the door to small investors. Most mutual funds, however, offer investment plans that allow investors to begin with a modest amount and add additional amounts periodically.

◆ Reinvestment Opportunity

In most mutual funds, income and capital gains distributions can be automatically reinvested. More than a convenience, this is a sound investment concept.

◆ Acceptability as Collateral

Normally, mutual fund investments are good collateral for a loan. Many types of investments may not be acceptable, either because the

Many investment options require a large initial investment, which closes the door to small investors.

bank is not familiar with the investment, the investment does not have sufficient liquidity, or the current value is not readily available. However, mutual funds are usually acceptable because they may be redeemed on demand and because they publish their value daily.

...common stock mutual funds may offer investors a reasonable inflation hedge over time, because the investment is not tied to the sinking value of a dollar...

◆ Current Information

Many investments provide little information after the original purchase is made, and the investor can only speculate as to the financial condition of the investment. A mutual fund, by law, must issue financial reports at regular intervals, disclosing full details regarding its holdings and its present condition. Current information is not only desirable, it should be insisted upon with any investment.

◆ Ease of Transfer

Mutual funds are often bought because their ownership is easily transferred from one person to another, unlike many other investment alternatives.

◆ Income Production

Mutual funds vary in the income they produce, depending on their investment objectives, but all funds pay an annual distribution of profits, when earned, and a distribution of any net income received from companies held in the portfolio. Some mutual funds maintain an objective of investing in common stocks that pay little or no dividends. These funds attempt to invest in companies that appreciate in value, rather than generate taxable dividends. Some funds offer "**check-a-month**" plans that provide monthly payments to you from your investment.

◆ Inflation Hedge

Owning shares in a common stock mutual fund whose objective is capital growth may offer investors a reasonable inflation hedge over time, because the investment is not tied to the sinking value of a dollar but to the value of growing companies.

(14-1)   *How Investments Compare Against "Ideal" Attributes Over Time*

Requisites of an Ideal Attribute Over Time	Stock Mutual Fund	Individual Common Stock	Fixed Income Mutual Fund	Individual Debt Security	Individual Real Estate	Fixed Insurance Annuity	Gold in Bars	Savings Account	Mortgage	Certificate of Deposit
Diversification	Yes	No	Yes	No	No	No	No	No	No	No
Record Keeping	Yes	No	Yes	No	No	No	No	Yes	Yes	Yes
Reinvestment Opportunities	Yes	*Maybe*	Yes	*Maybe*	No	No	No	Yes	No	Yes
Current Information	Yes	Yes	Yes	Yes	No	*Maybe*	Yes	Yes	Yes	Yes
Professional Management	Yes	No	Yes	No	No	Yes	No	Yes	No	Yes
Ease of Transfer	Yes	Yes	Yes	Yes	*Maybe*	*Maybe*	Yes	Yes	*Maybe*	Yes
Opportunity for Growth	Yes	Yes	*Maybe*	*Maybe*	Yes	No	Yes	No	No	No
Liquidity	Yes	Yes	Yes	Yes	No	*Maybe*	*Maybe*	Yes	No	*Maybe*
Available in Convenient Denominations	Yes	Yes	Yes	No	No	Yes	No	Yes	No	Yes
Inflation Hedge	Yes	Yes	No	No	*Maybe*	No	Yes	No	No	No
Income-Producing	*Maybe*	*Maybe*	Yes	Yes	*Maybe*	Yes	No	Yes	Yes	Yes
Acceptable as Collateral	Yes	Yes	Yes	Yes	Yes	Yes	Yes	Yes	*Maybe*	Yes
Limited Liability	Yes	Yes	Yes	Yes	Yes	Yes	Yes	Yes	Yes	Yes

The table above compares the attributes of an "ideal" investment with various types of investments.

My Beliefs About Mutual Funds

My Beliefs About Mutual Funds

All mutual funds are not equal –
some are better than others.

There are over 4,500 mutual funds. But just because an investment company offers a mutual fund that meets the criteria of an ideal investment doesn't necessarily mean it's a good fund in which to invest.

A combination of investment objectives, restrictions, performance, ethics, qualifications of the managers, dedication and support systems contributes dramatically to the differences among mutual funds. In theory, all mutual funds have access to the entire common stock and fixed income market, but not all are solid performers over time.

Many funds state similar investment objectives. In fact, many have the same investment philosophy, but very few have outstanding and consistent results over time.

It is important that you understand the investment philosophy, objectives and policies of any mutual fund in which you invest. Is the philosophy logical? Does it make sense? How does the fund intend to implement its investment philosophy? Does it follow its discipline consistently year after year, or does it change its approach frequently?

Most importantly, examine the investment results of the fund. What is the record of the investment manager? Has the fund been successful over time? Are the results consistent? How do the results compare with those funds with similar objectives?

Of course, the fact that a fund performed well in the past does not necessarily mean that it will in the future.

Equity Investments Over Time

It is my belief that the soundest and safest place for me to invest my own money is in mutual funds that are searching for and investing in companies with the characteristics that distinguish successful companies: earnings and revenues that are growing at an accelerating rate.

Why do I believe this?

- Successful companies have proven that they offer a unique, outstanding product or service which creates a strong demand.

- Such companies have demonstrated that they have the ability to sustain and increase profits by adjusting costs and even raising prices, thus compensating for the shrinking value of a dollar.

- Rising profits increase the demand for the companies' shares, keeping their market value higher than other less successful companies. **The greater the demand for shares,** the higher the market value.

When the train leaves the station, you need to be on it.

By owning an interest in a group of **successful companies** through a mutual fund, you have a real opportunity to stay ahead of the shrinking value of a dollar and to accumulate wealth.

Identifying such companies requires computer technology and the techniques of a sophisticated on-line data processing system – resources available to a good fund manager.

In addition, I strongly believe that the more successful investment managers **remain "fully invested,"** **instead of speculating with your money** by attempting to predict how much should be kept in cash while trying to predict which direction the market will go. If the investment manager remains fully invested, the fund is able to catch the upward spurts I described earlier. In other words, when the train leaves the station you need to be on it.

After decades of experience, it is my opinion that it is best to invest in companies paying little or no dividends. **Dividends are not as important as earnings. Earnings must come first**. A company must earn money before it should pay any dividends. However, before dividends can be paid to shareholders, taxes must be paid by the company on its earnings. If dividends are paid out by a company, they are in effect taxed twice because a tax is incurred first by the company and second by the shareholder. But if the earnings are kept by the company and not paid out in dividends, the money is taxed only once. In this case, the retained earnings can be put to work to generate more earnings, which in turn can further increase the value of the company. As the market value of companies in a specific fund increases, so does the value of the fund.

My $10,000 Invested in "Fund A"

To illustrate the principle that anyone can achieve financial independence, here is a real life example of my personal investing experience. On October 31, 1958, I invested $10,000 in a common stock mutual fund that I'll refer to as Fund A.

*I still own those shares today. From October 31, 1958 to December 31, 1993, my investment grew at an average rate of 14.6% a year. During that time there have been wars, severe inflation, recessions, and the famous October 1987 "correction." The value of my $10,000 investment has not grown at a constant rate over time; I did not expect that it would. In fact, it has fluctuated widely in price. However, **if** I had wanted to trade my investment back into dollars, I could have exchanged those shares for $1,209,766 on December 31, 1993.*

*When people hear of results such as these, they believe I was "lucky." They don't believe they could achieve such results themselves over time with similar investments. But who is to say they could not? Years ago, I was **absolutely** determined to achieve financial independence. I made my original investment of $10,000 and then remained patient, allowing time to work for me. No miracles were expected; I simply had the confidence in a fully-managed investment and believed in the power of compounding over time.*

From October 31, 1958 through December 31, 1993, the dollar lost 80% of its value at an average rate of 4.6% a year. Because of this, I could have traded my shares of Fund A for many more dollars in 1993 because the dollars were worth about one-fifth as much as they were in 1958. While I could have exchanged my shares for $1,209,766 on December 31, 1993, it should be understood that these 1993 dollars would actually buy only what $241,953 would have bought in 1958 (100% - 80% = 20% x $1,209,766 = $241,953). This bit of reality further underscores the importance of a growing investment that beats the continued shrinking value of a dollar.

I remained patient, allowing time to work for me.

Fixed Income Investments

When it comes to fixed income investments, my experience has shown that people are more interested in receiving the return OF their money than receiving a return ON their money.

In direct contrast to common stocks, which I consider to be long-term investments, fixed income securities are worthwhile investments for the short term.

This short-term limited risk is due to the nature of these investments. When you buy fixed income securities (bonds, for example), you are **lending** money to a company or to the government in exchange for interest payments.

Unlike common stocks, these "debt" securities do not represent ownership interests in a company; their value does not increase as the company's value increases, so long as interest rates remain unchanged. Because debt securities are tied to a dollar, they have not historically protected against the dollar's declining value over time to the extent that common stocks have.

A Potential Financial Risk

Financial institutions offering fixed income investments to the public are in competition with each other to attract dollars. The more money they can accumulate under their own management, the greater their profits. If the highest interest rate attracts the most money, many institutions will strive to provide the highest rate.

Within a specific investment sector, there is only a limited supply of quality investments available from which all institutions may choose. All investments of the same quality in a particular sector generally provide the same amount of yield or interest. So, if an institution wants to increase the yield on one of its products, it must increase the risk and buy lower quality investments. The competition to have the highest yield is so great that lower quality investments are sometimes used to gain a higher yield and, in so doing, the degree of risk is greatly increased.

Financial institutions ...are in competition with each other to attract dollars.

I believe most people are interested in receiving the highest yield possible, *but only from quality investments*. I do not believe people want to assume increased risk by owning lower-quality investments.

... periodic investing
enhances your
opportunity for
making a profit
over time.

The Amazing Results of Regular Investments

*When share prices vary up and down, periodic investing
enhances your opportunity for making a profit over time.*

You might think that since a certain investment did well in the past, it will do well in the future. But no one knows for certain. Even if you are optimistic and believe you will make a reasonable return on your investment, you still have the nagging question: What does the future offer?

Simply stated, only one of three things can happen to your investment. Your future results can only be:

> Identical to the past
> Better than the past
> Worse than the past

What Does the Future Offer?

Perhaps this question can be answered by studying the two assumed investments in Chart 16-1 – Investment **"A"** and Investment **"B."** Let's assume that for each investment, you make two decisions:

What does the
future offer?

1. You intend to invest $100 every month without fail

   and

2. You intend to do this for 10 years.

Obviously, the price per share of your investments could go either up or down. Chart 16-1 shows that in Investment **A** the price continually goes up, while in Investment **B** the price initially goes down, then later returns only to its starting point. These are deliberately exaggerated examples to illustrate a key concept about regular investing. They do not refer to a specific investment. Taxes have not been considered since they would only cloud the message.

First, with **A,** your investment starts at $6 a share and the price continues to increase every month, year after year, reaching $16 a share at the end of the tenth year. The price always goes up, never down in value. Under Investment **A**, you pay a slightly higher amount for a share each time you invest.

Second, in **B,** your investment starts at $6 a share, the same as **A,** but the price per share goes **down** for the first five years, to a low of $1.50 per share. Then, over the last five years, the price returns **only** to the **original price** of $6 a share. In other words, in **B,** the price continues to drop every month for the first five years, then increases for the last five years. The price per share starts at $6 a share and, after 10 long years, ends at only $6 a share. It is never higher.

(16-1)   *Share Prices for A and B*

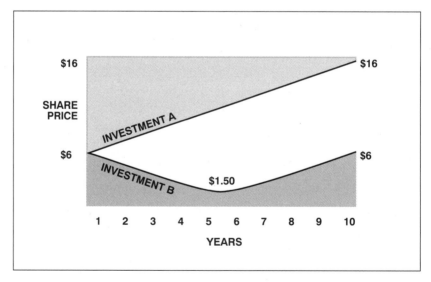

Assume you follow through with both of your intentions of (1) investing each and every month and (2) investing continuously for the full 10 years. Of these two investments, **A** and **B,** which would offer you the greatest opportunity for profit? Would the value of your investment be greater by following to completion **A** or **B** ? If you selected **A,** the obvious choice, you would have made money. But, as hard as it may be to believe, you would have done better if you had you followed Investment **B**.

Here is why. In either investment, you would have invested $100 each month, month after month, for 10 years. Therefore, you would have invested $1,200 each year or $12,000 in 10 years. At the end of 10 years, **A** would have been worth $18,919, while **B** would have been worth $24,130. Investment **B** would have been 40% more profitable than **A**.

Most people would naturally choose **A,** because they think the share price **must** go up regularly in order to make a profit. In **B,** the price did not always go up; rather, it went down for the first five years, providing the opportunity for **buying many more shares with your money**. Even though at maturity the price of each share in Investment **B** never exceeded the original price of $6 a share, at the end of 10 years **B** was the better investment. This is not magic. When the price of your shares was low, each of your $100 investments bought more shares. In fact during the 10 years, you accumulated over three times as many shares as in **A**.

...the price of your shares does not necessarily have to go up each month in order for you to have a profit.

Is there any probability of Investment **A** or **B** actually occurring? Probably not. Investing experience shows that reality is usually somewhere in between. The important point is that if you consistently invest at planned intervals over a sustained period of time, the price of your shares does not necessarily have to go up each month in order for you to have a profit. Certainly, if you were forced to liquidate your investment at a time when your shares were worth less than you paid for them, you would have a loss.

Again, the key message here is: **When share prices vary, periodic investing may reduce the average cost of a share and can enhance your potential for making a reasonable profit over time.**

Of course, a periodic investment plan does not guarantee a profit and will not prevent short-term losses in a declining market. However, it does offer a solid strategy for long-term investing.

What Happens in Between?

To continue this example, the results of Investments **A** and **B** could be seriously affected if they were terminated before 10 years. For example, selling any time in the first six years would assure a loss in **B** versus a smaller gain in Investment **A**.

(16-2)   *Results During 10-Year Period*

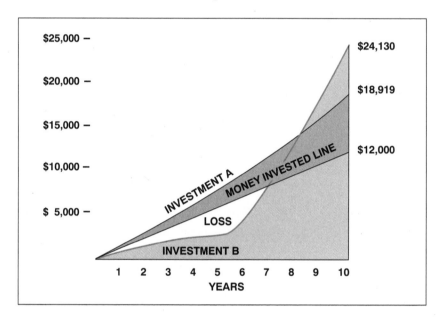

When you follow Investment **B** in the chart above, the line representing **B** is below the **Money Invested Line** for the first six years and eight months. Obviously, the greatest loss would have occurred at the end of the fifth year, when the price of the shares reached the lowest point. If you were forced to terminate your investment at this point, you would have suffered approximately a 50% loss. A short-term loss should not influence your thinking when you intend to invest over a long period, but it illustrates investment risks.

From the halfway point in this example, the line representing Investment **B** rapidly rises and crosses the **Money Invested Line** in less than two years from the low. If you were forced to terminate your investment at this point, you would realize a profit. Investment **B** continues to rise rapidly to become the more profitable investment at the end of 10 years. It is important for you to notice that for the first 97 months, the results of **A** would be greater than **B**. At the end of 10 years (120 months), however, Investment **B**, coming from behind, would be more profitable by a wide margin.

Again, these examples are based upon two assumptions:

1. You would have invested money each month, not missing a single month. **If you missed only one month, the results of both Investment A and B would be different.**

2. You were determined to invest your $100 a month for 10 years, not five years or eight years, but 10 years.

A short-term loss should not influence your thinking…

For simplicity, it was assumed there would be **no income** or earnings from either Investment **A** or **B**. Only the price per share varied up and down. If earnings or income had been considered and if they had been reinvested in additional shares each year, the results of both Investment **A** and **B** would have been greater at the end of 10 years.

◆ Another Possibility to Consider

Thus far, we have discussed the results of an investment of $100 a month for 10 years in Investment **A** and **B**. We also have reviewed what happens if you terminate either investment before completion. Now consider what would happen if you could no longer live up to your first goal – investing $100 each month – but you could achieve your other objective of leaving your money invested for the full 10 years.

Say you stopped investing at the end of the fifth year, when the price of your shares would be the lowest in Investment **B**. In this case, which plan would give you the greatest opportunity for profit at the end of 10 years – Investment **A** or **B**?

During the first five years, you would have invested a total of $6,000 in both Investments **A** and **B**. Without any additional investment after the fifth year, the worth of the shares you accumulated during the first five years increased substantially during the second five-year period (16-3).

(16-3)   *Results if Forced to Discontinue Investing*

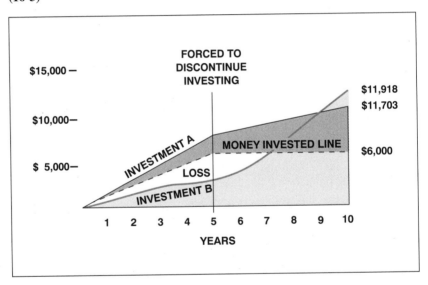

At the end of 10 years, the total worth of Investments **A** and **B** would be approximately the same. Investment **A** would be worth $11,703; **B** would be worth $11,918. Note that in this assumed example, using this extreme case, the worth of the investment at the end of 10 years is approximately two times the $6,000 originally invested.

You invested each month during the first five years a total of $6,000, then stopped. What happened to your investment?

Referring to Chart 16-3, the broken line is the **Money Invested Line** that represents your cost. This line increases for the first five years to $6,000 and then is level from the fifth year to the tenth year. You invested $100 a month for the first five years, then discontinued all investing from the fifth year on.

The line representing Investment **A is always above the Money Invested Line,** so that if you terminated your investment at any time, you would have realized a profit in this hypothetical example. If you had followed Investment **B** and terminated your investment before the seventh year, you would have suffered a loss. This loss would vary in size, depending upon when you were forced to sell. The greatest loss would occur at the end of the fifth year. Investment **B** becomes profitable after seven years, one month. The amount of the profit increases rapidly to the tenth year.

Why did Investment **B** do so well at the end of 10 years? It is simple. Again, when the price of the shares was low, each of your $100 investments bought more shares. By the end of the fifth year, you would have accumulated over 2½ times as many shares as in Investment **A**. **As the price of the shares increased, your potential loss rapidly changed to profit.**

We have taken two hypothetical examples, Investments **A** and **B**, and studied them from different investment perspectives. You obviously know you will make money in an investment if the price continues upward, as in Investment **A**. I hope these hypothetical examples have increased your understanding of the real probability of making money over time, even if the price fluctuates as it did in Investment **B**.

These illustrations show that you have an opportunity to become more financially secure if you follow through with a program of investing each month for a committed period of time.

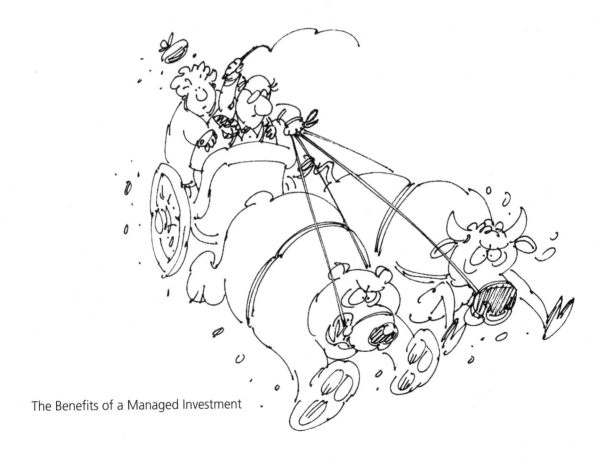

The Benefits of a Managed Investment

The Benefits of a Managed Investment

*Professional investment management
can add real value.*

The examples in Chapter 13 show the results of an unmanaged assumed investment in the Dow Jones Industrial Average over varying periods of time covering a total of 97 years. Now let's compare the potential added value that professional management can offer. Although there is no guarantee that a managed investment will outperform unmanaged investments, this illustration shows the potential of a managed investment.

For a managed investment, let us study the results of "Fund A" – the previous example from my personal investing experience.

First, a little information regarding the fund: This particular fund's investment objective is to seek capital growth by investing primarily in common stocks that are considered to have better than average prospects for appreciation. The fund's investment management team searches for successful companies whose earnings and revenues are believed to be growing at an accelerated rate. These companies are **not required** to pay dividends.

The mutual fund's investment management team searches for successful companies whose earnings and revenues are believed to be growing...

The following guidelines have been used for this study:

It encompassed 22.75 years, from July 1, 1971, through March 31, 1994.

Multiple "rolling" periods are covered: one-, three-, five-, 10-, 15- and 20-year durations.

The starting point of the first investment period began the first day of July 1971 and lasted the duration of one of the multiple periods (one, three, five, 10, 15, 20 years). The next investment period started at the beginning of the second quarter (October 1971) and also lasted the duration of one of the multiple periods. This process continued to advance one quarter of a year at a time until the last investment period ended on March 31, 1994.

There were 88 one-year investment periods during 22.75 years. There were only twelve 20-year periods.

One-Time Investment of $10,000

In this segment, let's assume that $10,000 was traded for shares of Fund A, a fully-managed no-load (no sales charges) common stock mutual fund. At the beginning of each period considered, assume that a one-time investment was made on the first business day of that quarter. All dividends from investment income and distributions from realized profits were reinvested in additional shares.

At the end of each period, the accumulated shares of Fund A were traded back into dollars. Each investment started with $10,000 and each period ended with a certain dollar value. The difference between these two figures was converted to an average annual percentage return. The individual percentage returns were then listed in order of value from the highest to the lowest as in prior examples.

For comparison, two different **unmanaged** investments were made with the same amounts and over the same periods of time. One was a hypothetical investment in the Dow Jones Industrial Average. The other hypothetical investment was in the Standard & Poor's 500 Index (S&P 500). This latter index is an unmanaged group of 500 stocks, which many consider to be more representative of the stock market in general than the Dow Jones Industrial Average. No expenses or fees are reflected in either the Dow or the S&P 500 results. Management and service fees and brokerage expenses are, however, deducted from the fully-managed investment in Fund A, naturally reducing its results. No taxes are reflected in any of the investment results.

The results are presented using two different methods. The first is illustrated with charts. The second uses tables that show the probability of receiving a certain percentage return. The original concept of the

(17-1)   *$10,000 Investments in "Fund A"*

(With All Dividends Reinvested)

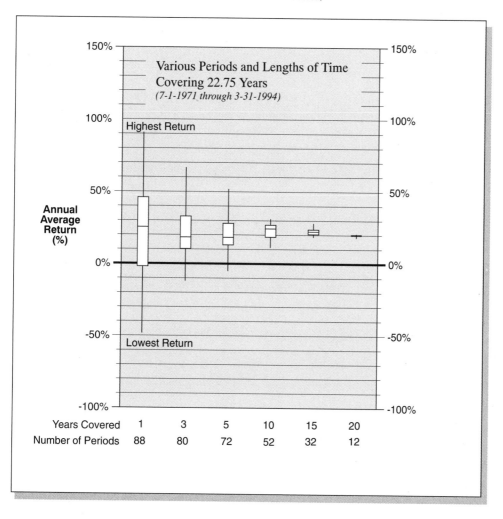

charts is fully explained in Chapter 13 (Charts 13-5, 13-6A, and 13-6B).

I have selected a small number of representative charts to help you understand the actual investment results of Fund A. (A complete set of charts for all three investments can be found in Addendum B.)

In Chart 17-1, the various periods of Fund A have been drawn to scale and can be compared with one another. Clearly, the extreme spread of percentage values from the highest return to the lowest return for each individual period narrowed rapidly from the one-year results through the 20-year results. The total percentage spread of one-year results was 139%, from a high of 91% to a low of minus 48%. By comparison, the 20-year total spread was much less, amounting to only 3.3%, with a high of 21.5% to a low of 18.2%.

The **Middle 50% of Results** for a one-year period fell between a high of 45% and a low of minus 1.5%, or a total spread of 47%. The spread for the **Middle 50% of Results** of the 15-year period was reduced to only 3.1%, ranging from a high of 23.4% to a low of 20.2%.

Comparable charts of the Dow Jones and S&P 500 are found in Addendum B.

Table 17-2 compares the **percentage spreads** (the range from the highest return for any given period to the lowest return) of the overall

(17-2)   *Comparing the Percentage Spreads of the Overall Results*
($10,000 Investments 7-1-1971 through 3-31-1994)

	One-Year Periods			20-Year Periods		
	Spread	*around*	**Mid-Value**	**Spread**	*around*	**Mid-Value**
"Fund A"	139%	*around*	23.0%	3.3%	*around*	19.6%
Dow	93%	*around*	11.7%	1.7%	*around*	11.6%
S&P 500	101%	*around*	12.5%	1.5%	*around*	11.6%

results of Fund A (a fully-managed investment) to those of the Dow and
S&P 500 (unmanaged investments). The total spreads are greater for Fund A
than the other two, but you should note how much higher the Mid-Value
is for Fund A when compared with the Mid-Value for the Dow and the
S&P 500. In each case, the spread is around the Mid-Value.

The fully-managed
fund in time pulled
away from the
two unmanaged
investments.

Comparing Identical Period Charts

Addendum B contains the individual charts of the three different
investments drawn to scale for each one of the separate five-year periods
so they can be easily compared. (See Charts B10 through B15 for more
information.)

The most significant of these charts, B15, is repeated as Chart 17-3
on page 164. Observe how the results of the fully-managed fund in time
pulled away from the other two unmanaged investments. The lowest result
of Fund A was higher than even the highest results of the other two.

(17-3)

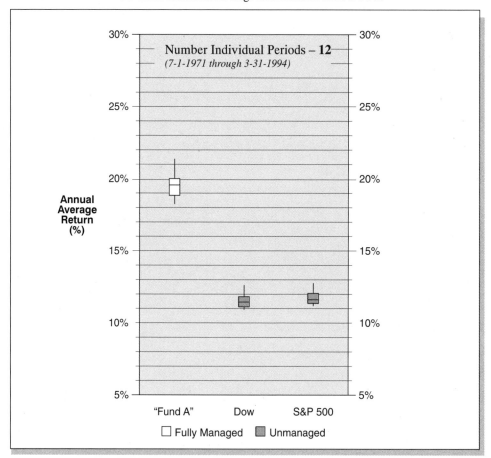

20-Year Results
$10,000 One-Time Investment
(With All Dividends Reinvested)
Results of "Fund A" compared with the results of
Dow Jones Industrial Average and Standard & Poor's 500

Number Individual Periods – **12**
(7-1-1971 through 3-31-1994)

Annual Average Return (%)

"Fund A"   Dow   S&P 500

☐ Fully Managed   ▨ Unmanaged

   The Mid-Value for Fund A was 19.61%, which was much higher than the other two. The Dow was 11.59%, and the S&P 500 was 11.64%. During this 20-year period, it is interesting to note that the dollar lost a total of 70% of its value at the annual rate of 6%.

(17-4A)

The Probabilities of Receiving a Certain Return
$10,000 One-Time Investment
(With All Dividends Reinvested)

Comparing "Fund A" results with those of Dow Jones Industrial Average and Standard & Poor's 500

Covering 22.75 Years (7-1-1971 through 3-31-1994)
*Percentage Results **in Excess of** Various Compound Rates*

"Fund A"

PERIOD (YEARS)	0%	2%	4%	6%	8%	10%	12%	14%	16%	18%	20%	22%	24%	26%	28%	30%	NUMBER OF PERIODS
1	72	72	67	65	64	61	60	57	57	54	53	51	50	46	42	39	88
3	91	90	87	87	83	77	71	67	60	50	46	41	35	31	30	27	80
5	100	100	100	97	94	88	81	72	62	54	44	37	33	31	25	23	72
10	100	100	100	100	100	100	98	88	82	75	57	46	42	28	15	3	52
15	100	100	100	100	100	100	100	100	100	100	78	59	18	6	3	0	32
20	100	100	100	100	100	100	100	100	(100)	33	0	0	0	0	0	0	12

Dow Jones Industrial Average

PERIOD (YEARS)	0%	2%	4%	6%	8%	10%	12%	14%	16%	18%	20%	22%	24%	26%	28%	30%	NUMBER OF PERIODS
1	72	71	67	64	60	53	48	44	39	37	32	28	27	22	20	19	88
3	91	85	81	75	70	61	51	45	36	26	17	6	5	3	3	3	80
5	100	97	84	77	69	65	59	48	27	19	15	8	4	4	4	1	72
10	100	100	96	86	84	75	65	55	32	13	0	0	0	0	0	0	52
15	100	100	100	100	100	93	71	34	3	0	0	0	0	0	0	0	32
20	100	100	100	100	100	(100)	25	0	0	0	0	0	0	0	0	0	12

Standard & Poor's 500

PERIOD (YEARS)	0%	2%	4%	6%	8%	10%	12%	14%	16%	18%	20%	22%	24%	26%	28%	30%	NUMBER OF PERIODS
1	77	71	70	69	62	60	54	48	42	38	30	26	25	22	21	18	88
3	91	88	87	81	73	62	53	46	38	23	12	6	5	5	2	1	80
5	98	95	90	84	79	70	63	56	27	13	8	4	4	4	1	0	72
10	100	100	100	94	86	82	75	61	34	3	0	0	0	0	0	0	52
15	100	100	100	100	100	96	75	50	9	0	0	0	0	0	0	0	32
20	100	100	100	100	100	(100)	33	0	0	0	0	0	0	0	0	0	12

(100) Represents the highest rate of return occurring for **all** the 20-year investment periods.

The table shown on the preceding page illustrates the same information in a different way, when a fully-managed investment is compared with the results of two unmanaged investments. Compare the probability of receiving greater than 0% interest with each investment. Also, compare what the probability was of receiving more than 6%. What were the chances of receiving more than 14%? Was the probability greater with the fully-managed investment?

Chart 17-4B, on the following page, was created by using the probability data from the 16% columns in Table 17-4A. This three-dimensional view helps you visualize how the probabilities of the three investments (Fund A, the Dow and the S&P 500) compare with each other over different periods of time. Note the dramatic differences between a fully-managed fund and unmanaged investments.

It is important to keep in mind that all of the results of Fund A have been relatively understated because each year a service cost, an investment management fee and trading commissions were deducted from the results. On the other hand, no expenses of any kind are reflected in the Dow or S&P 500 results. If applicable fees **had** been deducted from the Dow's and S&P 500's results, the difference in performance would have been even greater.

Professional investment management can lead to real value.

(17-4B)   *The Probabilities of Receiving a 16% Return*
                    $10,000 One-Time Investment

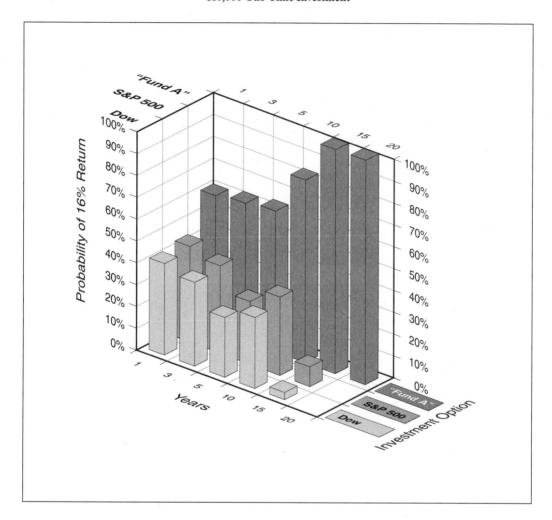

An Investment of $100 a Month

This segment covers an investment of $100 a month with all dividends reinvested in Fund A, the Dow and the S&P 500. The same assumptions stated for the one-time $10,000 investment apply to this segment.

I have selected certain charts on all three $100 investments to demonstrate the results of this study. A complete set for all three investments can be found in Addendum C.

Compare the differences and similarities in the chart below with the $10,000 investments shown in Chart 17-1.

(17-5)   *$100-a-Month Investments in "Fund A"*
(With All Dividends Reinvested)

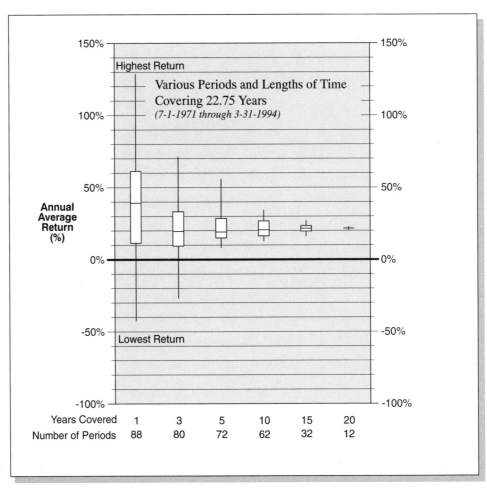

Compare the percentage spreads of the overall results in the $100-a-month investment in the chart below with the same information in the $10,000 investments in Chart 17-2.

(17-6)   *Comparing the Percentage Spreads of the Overall Results*
         ($100-a-Month Investments 7-1-1971 through 3-31-1994)

	One-Year Periods			20-Year Periods		
	Spread	*around*	**Mid-Value**	**Spread**	*around*	**Mid-Value**
"Fund A"	171%	*around*	40.0%	2.6%	*around*	21.1%
Dow	109%	*around*	14.5%	1.0%	*around*	14.2%
S&P 500	105%	*around*	13.5%	0.9%	*around*	14.3%

Addendum C contains the individual charts of the three different investments drawn to scale for each of the separate periods so that they can be easily compared with one another. (See Charts C10 through C15 for more information.)

The most important of those charts (C15) is repeated on the next page as Chart 17-7. Again, notice that the investment results of the fully-managed Fund A are significantly higher than the best results of the other two unmanaged investments. There were twelve "rolling" 20-year period results in the 22.75 years ending March 31, 1994. The Mid-Value of Fund A was 21.1% – a much higher rate than the other two unmanaged investments. The Dow was 14.2% and the S&P 500 was 14.3%. By way of comparison during this 20-year period, the dollar lost a total of 70% of its value at the rate of 6% a year.

(17-7)

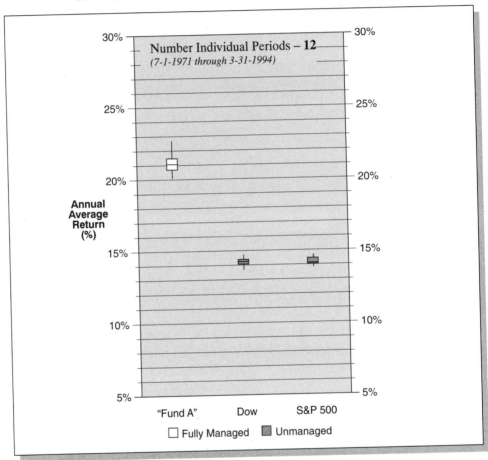

20-Year Results
$100 a Month
(With All Dividends Reinvested)
Results of "Fund A" compared with the results of
Dow Jones Industrial Average and Standard & Poor's 500

The table on the next page shows the same information regarding a $100-a-month investment. It illustrates the probability of receiving a certain return.

(17-8A)

The Probabilities of Receiving a Certain Return
$100-a-Month Investment
(With All Dividends Reinvested)

Comparing "Fund A" results with those of Dow Jones Industrial Average and Standard & Poor's 500

Covering 22.75 Years (7-1-1971 through 3-31-1994)
*Percentage Results **in Excess of** Various Compound Rates*

"Fund A"

PERIOD (YEARS)	0%	2%	4%	6%	8%	10%	12%	14%	16%	18%	20%	22%	24%	26%	28%	30%	NUMBER OF PERIODS
1	84	84	82	80	80	78	75	73	71	69	64	62	60	59	57	55	88
3	95	95	92	90	86	75	70	66	62	53	48	47	45	40	35	35	80
5	100	100	100	100	100	94	86	81	68	59	47	43	36	31	27	23	72
10	100	100	100	100	100	100	100	96	78	57	51	50	44	26	17	13	52
15	100	100	100	100	100	100	100	100	96	84	65	50	15	6	0	0	32
20	100	100	100	100	100	100	100	100	100	100	(100)	8	0	0	0	0	12

Dow Jones Industrial Average

PERIOD (YEARS)	0%	2%	4%	6%	8%	10%	12%	14%	16%	18%	20%	22%	24%	26%	28%	30%	NUMBER OF PERIODS
1	76	73	71	67	64	61	55	51	43	39	31	23	22	21	17	13	88
3	92	86	82	77	72	66	56	43	32	22	15	13	10	7	6	6	80
5	100	98	95	86	75	70	59	47	33	22	12	9	6	6	4	2	72
10	100	100	100	92	88	86	75	65	48	17	5	1	0	0	0	0	52
15	100	100	100	100	100	100	100	87	37	0	0	0	0	0	0	0	32
20	100	100	100	100	100	100	(100)	83	0	0	0	0	0	0	0	0	12

Standard & Poor's 500

PERIOD (YEARS)	0%	2%	4%	6%	8%	10%	12%	14%	16%	18%	20%	22%	24%	26%	28%	30%	NUMBER OF PERIODS
1	78	73	71	70	69	59	55	45	42	36	34	29	27	26	20	18	88
3	92	90	87	80	76	64	56	49	40	26	22	12	9	7	5	4	80
5	100	100	98	94	84	73	65	51	26	16	12	6	6	4	0	0	72
10	100	100	100	100	94	90	86	71	40	13	5	0	0	0	0	0	52
15	100	100	100	100	100	100	100	93	21	0	0	0	0	0	0	0	32
20	100	100	100	100	100	100	(100)	91	0	0	0	0	0	0	0	0	12

(100) Represents the highest rate of return occurring for **all** the 20-year investment periods.

Relate Table 17-8A on the preceding page to the probabilities of receiving a certain return on $10,000 one-time investments (Table 17-4A).

Again, it is interesting to observe that the probability of receiving a higher percentage return is generally a little greater for all three $100-a-month investments, when compared with a corresponding one-time $10,000 investment.

(17-8B)

The Probabilities of Receiving a 16% Return
$100-a-Month Investment

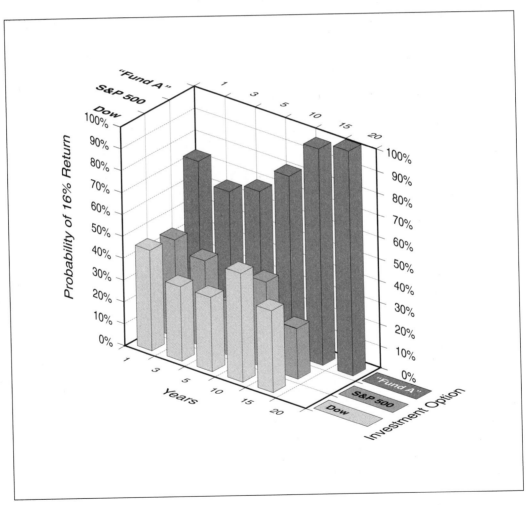

The probability data from the 16% columns in Table 17-8A, under Fund A, the Dow and the S&P 500, was used to create the three-dimensional Chart 17-8B shown on the opposite page. This was done to help you visualize how the probabilities of the three investments compare with each other over different periods of time. Note the dramatic differences between this fully-managed fund and unmanaged investments.

It is important to note that historically many fully-managed funds have not outperformed unmanaged investments. However, professional investment management can lead to real value.

Think twice about borrowing money to invest if you
do not have the means to pay it back at any time.

Borrowing Money to Invest

Banks are willing to lend you an umbrella,
but when it starts to rain, they may
ask for the umbrella back.

When you borrow to invest, you use somebody else's money to leverage your opportunity to make a profit. Obviously, when you do this, you must pay interest for the use of the money. While you increase your opportunity for profit by borrowing, you also increase your risk for loss.

Some of the reasons you might borrow to invest:

> For improving your financial position – learning new skills or investing in equipment to improve your future income or security

> For your own business – this investment is under your control and you leverage your capital to increase your profit potential

> For owning securities for long-term growth

> For owning a home which provides shelter, a long-term investment, and possible tax advantages

What is the degree of risk involved when borrowing or not borrowing?

Let us assume you made two $10,000 investments using two strategies:

> **Strategy A – Not borrowing** money

> **Strategy B – Borrowing** money

Let's also assume each strategy could have produced three different results. Your investment:

> Doubled – by 100% (upside opportunity)

> Lost 25% (downside risk)

> Lost 50% (greater downside risk)

Now let's compare the results of the two strategies and their different effects.

Strategy A – Not borrowing money

Upside opportunity:
Over Time
$10,000 grew to $20,000 . . . .= 100% profit

Two downside risks:
Over Time
$10,000 fell to $7,500 . . . .=   25% loss
Over Time
$10,000 fell to $5,000 . . . .=   50% loss

Strategy B – Borrowing money *

You borrowed 75% of $10,000   **$ 7,500**
You personally invested 25%   **2,500**
                                     _____
                                  $10,000

Upside opportunity:
Over Time
$10,000 grew to $20,000
  $20,000 minus borrowed $7,500 = $12,500
  $2,500 invested grew to $12,500 . . . .= 400% profit

Two downside risks:
Over Time
$10,000 fell to $7,500
  $7,500 minus borrowed $7,500 = 0
  $2,500 invested fell to $0 . . . .= 100% loss
Over Time
$10,000 fell to $5,000
  $5,000 minus borrowed $7,500 = - $2,500
  $2,500 invested fell to - $2,500 . . . .= 200% loss

The cost of borrowing is not taken into consideration.

You can see that borrowing money to invest can greatly increase your opportunity for profit (400% in this case), but your risk for loss is also potentially magnified (a 200% loss).

If you borrowed the money from a bank and your collateral fell in value, the bank would likely demand more collateral to cover the loan. If you failed to add collateral, part of your investment could be sold and the proceeds used to repay part or all of the loan. If the bank did not receive enough proceeds from the sale of your investment, it would expect you to cover the loss.

If your bank becomes worried about your financial condition, it will likely "call your loan" (force you to pay it back). In other words, banks are willing to lend you an umbrella, but when it starts to rain, they may ask for the umbrella back.

Banks are willing to lend you an umbrella, but when it starts to rain, they may ask for the umbrella back.

Think Twice About Borrowing Money

Previously, I explained how I "traded" $10,000 for shares of Fund A in October 1958 to help start the mutual fund. On December 31, 1993, I could have traded those accumulated shares back into $1,209,766 (but I didn't).

What I haven't told you is that in October 1958, I felt I didn't have enough dollars to comfortably invest the entire $10,000. I invested $2,500 of my own money and borrowed $7,500 from a bank to complete my initial $10,000 investment. In fact, I still owe the bank the original $7,500. I have paid the interest on the loan all these years; but after 35 years, I have not repaid the loan. Frankly, I have chosen not to repay it in order to demonstrate the concept of borrowing to invest over a long period of time.

In 1958 I faced two different risks: one, the amount borrowed represented a sizable personal risk, and two, when I invested, the market was not at a relative low point.

The motive behind my borrowing money was to convince my associates of my strong belief in the future of our fund.

The motive behind my borrowing money to invest in our new fund was **much stronger than profit**. I wanted to convince my associates and future investors of my strong belief in the future of our fund, and in my philosophy which has guided its growth since 1958.

I am **not** advocating the principle of borrowing money to invest, but it's an option you can and no doubt will use (at least for your home). Clearly, you must evaluate the risks and rewards associated with such "leverage." Weigh all factors and risks before making your decision.

> **Think twice about borrowing money**
> **if you do not have the means**
> **to *pay it back at any time*.**

PART 5

Becoming Financially Independent

How Do You Achieve Financial Independence?

How Do You Achieve Financial Independence?

It isn't so bad to be old OR poor,
  but it's a tragedy to be old AND poor.

During your lifetime, you will earn a sizable fortune. What you do with your savings determines how much you will accumulate. **Regardless of how much you earn, only what you save is really yours. You can always spend what you save, but you can never save what you spend**.

Consider each of the following questions carefully. The choices you make can determine whether or not you will be on the road to financial independence.

- Can you live within your earned income?
- Have you built an emergency reserve?
- Should you consider borrowing?
- Do you want to achieve financial independence?
- Are you **absolutely** determined to accomplish your financial goals?

Can You Live Within Your Earned Income?

The fundamental decision you must make is **whether or not you intend to live within your income**. If you decide to do this, it means you cannot spend more money than you earn. Frankly, this is going to take a **real** commitment on your part. You realize you can't have everything in life. You are forced to make choices. Which of your wants do you desire the most?

The fundamental decision you must make is whether or not you intend to live within your income.

**If you want something badly enough,
isn't it worth doing without something else now,
so you can acquire what you really want later?**

Living on One Income

At the time of our marriage, both my wife, Virginia, and I worked. She was a registered nurse training to become an anesthetist; I was beginning my career in the investment business.

*We both had a strong desire to raise a family, and we were worried about the consequences of getting accustomed to a lifestyle dependent on two incomes. We felt that if my wife had to reduce her work schedule, we might have trouble adjusting to that smaller income. Because of this possibility, **we decided we would live on only my earnings**, while saving and investing all of my wife's salary.*

This decision proved to be the right one for us as each of our four children came into our lives. We were not subjected to the emotional shock of being forced to drastically reduce our standard of living.

Have you built an emergency reserve?

Have You Built an Emergency Reserve?

As I have stated before, having an emergency reserve is prudent. How big should your emergency reserve be? Again, the customary **recommendation** is that you have three to six months of living costs in a "safe" bank account or fixed income investment. You may be in a unique situation where you wish to have more than six months' worth of emergency reserve so that you can sleep more easily at night. In my opinion, however, having a large reserve would not be wise. Can anyone afford, over time, to keep an excessive amount of money tied to the shrinking value of a dollar? I have always felt that I couldn't. I doubt you can, either.

Should You Consider Borrowing?

Try to develop a personal strategy about borrowing. It is an important financial decision that may involve a great deal of money.

Our Belief About Borrowing

*When my wife and I were first married, we agreed we would **never borrow money** except to buy a home or to leverage our investments. We never borrowed money even to buy a car. We never borrowed money to buy anything else that would commit us to spending our future income. We have never used credit cards to borrow money. We do use them, of course, but only as a convenience. As I mentioned earlier, if we wanted something badly enough, we saved until we had enough money to pay cash for it. But it wasn't as though we were not tempted.*

For example, in 1955, when a friend had borrowed money to buy a new car, we were still driving our 1949 Mercury convertible. Even though we kept the car in excellent condition, it was getting older and looked dated. We thought many times about selling some of our investments to buy a new car. But our desire to be financially independent was much stronger than our desire to keep up with others. We felt satisfied with our decision when we thought about the enormous loss in value our friend took in depreciation at the end of the year when new models were introduced. Our car lost only a little value but kept chugging along. We stayed on track toward our goal of becoming financially independent.

Do You Want to Achieve Financial Independence?

When you retire, will your relatives and friends be interested in knowing what kind of car you drove, in what kind of house you lived, who tailored your clothes, or to what clubs you belonged? Or, will they be interested in knowing that you can afford to live in comfort for the rest of your life?

You must decide what you want most. If you are determined to become financially independent, it is really quite simple:

Spend less than you earn, or make more than you spend, and wisely invest the difference.

Some people... will receive an unexpected windfall.

Are You Absolutely Determined to Accomplish Your Financial Goals?

Some people will inherit a sizable sum of money; some will receive an unexpected windfall. If you are like most people, however, your future will depend mainly on what **you do** for yourself.

If you decide to spend less than you earn, it should not be done just to save money. It should be done with the goal of becoming financially independent. **After you have determined what you want to do, make a firm commitment to yourself to do it**.

If you decide to save part of what you earn, will you still be able to maintain your current standard of living? Frankly, you may be forced to lower your standard of living slightly in order to accomplish your goals. Are you prepared for this possibility? You can easily find out by re-examining your priorities. It takes a certain amount of money to exist. It takes more for comfort, and it takes much more for luxury.

You cannot accomplish your goal of achieving financial indepen-

dence by wishing. It takes doing. It takes being committed and being absolutely determined to act.

What Do You Have to Do?

If you have decided that you truly want to achieve financial independence, here are some steps to follow:
- **Pay Yourself First**
- **Invest Wisely**
- **Remember the Value of Time**
- **Fight the Temptation to Spend What You Have Saved**
- **Try to Get Your Money's Worth**
- **Try to Buy Only What You Intend to Use**

• Pay Yourself First

Invest regularly – dollar by dollar.

Consider every month a loss unless you have saved a portion of your income.

Consider every month a loss unless you have saved a portion of your income.

Think of saving and then investing as your most important obligation each month, even ahead of paying your rent or mortgage.

Set aside a definite amount at the beginning of each month. How much should you set aside? A simple rule of thumb is at least 10% of your gross income invested for the long term.

An Important Point to Keep in Mind

If a dollar were to lose 6.7% of its value in a year, you cannot offset this loss in value by investing your money at only 6.7%. Mathematically, you must earn 7.18% on your investment just to keep up with a 6.7% annual loss in value of a dollar. As I have said before, if a dollar loses 6.7% each year for 10 years it will lose half its value.

... if a dollar loses 6.7% each year for 10 years it will lose half its value.

If you are having difficulty saving because of an outstanding or a growing loan balance on your credit cards, it may be necessary for you to literally cut up those cards and pay cash for everything you buy. This is an extreme form of self-discipline, but for some it may take drastic action. Whatever you do, make sure you don't plan to save only what is **left over** at the end of the month. Most likely, there won't be anything left.

◆ Invest Wisely

I have never told anyone what they **should do** with their money. Rather, I try to let people know **what they CAN do**. Ultimately, you must make up your own mind about **what YOU WANT to do.**

It would be wise to have your investments diversified, readily marketable and managed by professionals.

Again, one of the biggest financial risks you may face over the long term is the loss in value of a dollar. As I have said before, you would be wise to plan for the worst probability that a dollar may very likely lose one-half of its value every 10 years. If that occurs, it means that all of your investments will have to at least double in value during that time just to keep pace with the loss in dollar value (again, an average of 7.18% each year). Wherever you invest your money, it should have an opportunity to keep pace with and even earn more than the erosion in value of a dollar. Can you afford to invest for the long term in anything that **is tied** to a dollar, such as bonds, insurance and certificates of deposit?

The best time to plant an oak was 20 years ago. The second best time is now.

◆ Remember the Value of Time

Be patient. When you plant an acorn, you don't expect a sturdy oak in a year or two. It must be nourished and it takes TIME to grow. TIME can be your greatest asset if you start early. If you delay, TIME can be your greatest handicap.

...would you rather begin at age 20 and make small monthly investments or would you rather wait to age 40 and be forced to invest almost eight times as much each month?

The best time to plant an oak was 20 years ago. The second best time is now.

Today, you have more time remaining than you will ever have again. If you utilize the time you have remaining, you may increase the likelihood of winning the marathon challenge of achieving financial independence. If you get off to an early start, it will take less money to achieve your financial goal, because your money will be at work for you over a longer period. This provides you with a compounding advantage. For example, to accomplish the same financial goal at age 65, would you rather begin at age 20 and make small monthly investments or would you rather wait to age 40 and be forced to invest almost eight times as much each month? (Refer to Chart 4-3 using 10% rate of return.)

Look at "Value of Time" in your Stowers Financial Analysis.

One final point on the importance of time: It also allows you to overcome errors in judgment made along the way.

◆ Fight the Temptation to Spend What You Have Saved

Try to develop the willpower not to touch your long-term investments. Keep in mind that these investments are for your future financial independence. Try to leave them alone. When your initial savings reach a sizable sum, there is a great temptation to spend some of it. You can usually find some logical reason to justify the spending. Fight it.

Falling to Temptation

While I was in college, I used a motor scooter for transportation. Some of my professors thought it was unbecoming for a future executive to ride around on a motor scooter. Their comments upset me and, besides, I got wet when it rained. Eventually, I convinced myself that I should trade in the motor scooter for a new 1949 Mercury convertible. The additional cash I paid for the car came from redeeming those savings bonds I described earlier. In retrospect, I learned firsthand how easy it is to give in to temptation and justify spending money I had saved. I kept that car for a long time.

I learned firsthand how easy it is to give in to temptation and justify spending money I had saved.

◆ Try to Get Your Money's Worth

If you have a question about how much you should pay for something, just remember that it is worth only what someone else is willing to pay for it. How can you arrive at the correct amount? Take time to determine what you believe you could sell it for if you owned it.

...I looked at a used 1958 Cadillac with all the bells and whistles on it.

Getting My Money's Worth

In 1957 I was still driving my 1949 Mercury convertible. At that time several people made comments that my car did not reflect the successful image of someone in the investment business. It was too old. In response, I bought a new "ageless" Volkswagen Beetle. By 1959 people were again making comments such as, "If you are truly successful, why are you driving around in a Bug?" I thought these comments deserved further action, so I looked at a fancy used 1958 Cadillac Fleetwood with all the bells and whistles on it. I was determined not to pay any more for it than I believed I could sell it for. I remember paying the Cadillac dealer $2,500 for a car that someone else had purchased for $8,400 only a year ear-

lier. The reason I was able to pay this little was because the car had a new feature, "airride," which had potential problems. It glided on airbags filled with compressed air instead of normal springs and, as with any new technology, there were some bugs. For example, the air pump kept wearing out, but this potential problem did not discourage me. When I drove that wonderful-riding, long-finned car all comments ceased. I kept that Cadillac for five years, drove it thousands of miles, then sold it outright for the same price I originally paid for it – $2,500.

*My uncle used to say, **"Well bought; half sold."***

*I say, **"Well built; half sold."***

◆ Try to Buy Only What You Intend to Use

If you spend money for something you never use, obviously that money could have been better utilized another way. For example, it could be used as an additional investment toward your financial future.

The Most Expensive Dress My Wife Ever Bought

Several years ago, while we were in Boston, we went shopping at the famous Filene's Basement. My wife found a beautiful designer dress that had been marked down to $70 from over $700. She noticed on the price tag that the dress would be further reduced to $35 the following day – provided it had not been purchased by someone else.

*Virginia decided to take a chance and wait one more day. The next day we made a special trip to see if the dress was still there. To our surprise it was still on the rack. She bought the dress for $35, **took it home, but as it turns out she has never worn it.***

Bargains are not really bargains if they are never used.

At this point, you might think you can't afford to:

Live within your earned income,

Build an emergency reserve,

Avoid borrowing,

Save and invest for your future,

but

if you truly want to become financially independent,

ask yourself this question:

"Can I afford NOT to do this?"

If your commitment wavers, remember:

It isn't so bad to be old OR poor,

but it is a tragedy to be old AND poor.

Is this man fishing because he wants to ...

... or because he has to?

Where Can You Find Money To Invest?

Where Can You Find Money to Invest?

*You can always find extra money to set aside
if you are determined to do so.*

If, after reading the preceding chapters, you are determined to achieve financial independence, you are probably asking yourself, "How can I set aside money when I can barely make ends meet now?" You probably have the means if you take a closer look.

There are many ways of finding money to set aside:

- **Making Better Use of Your Time**
- **Working Even Harder to Do a Better Job**
- **Getting Your Money's Worth**
- **Planning for Financial Windfalls**
- **Trying Other Ways to Find Extra Money**

◆ Making Better Use of Your Time

Time is money. The efficient use of time can ultimately result in finding money to save. Make a record of exactly how you spend each minute of the day – from the time you get up until the time you go to bed at night. Keep a record for an entire month. At the end of the month, analyze exactly how you spent your time. Determine how much time was spent on each activity. Study the results. Were you satisfied with how you spent your time? Perhaps you could earn more money by simply making better use of your time.

Make a record of exactly how you spend each minute of the day…

◆ Working Even Harder to Do a Better Job

Are you convinced that you are making your best effort? Do you feel you are an expert at what you do? Can **anyone else** do your job better? Is there any way you could perform better? Are you proud of what you have done and are able to do? Do you believe you have convinced others that you have done your best?

The greatest test of all is to stand in front of a mirror and ask yourself, **"Can I honestly say, I have tried my very best?"**

◆ Getting Your Money's Worth

The process described below will help you find extra money. It is simple, effective and enlightening, and was **instrumental in improving my financial position.**

Our Important Message

*One of the most valuable exercises that my wife, Virginia, and I followed in our effort to improve our financial position was trying to continually convince ourselves that we were absolutely satisfied with the way we were spending our money. We wanted to get our money's worth. **I can't emphasize how important this was.***

Keep a daily record of how you spend money. List exactly **what** you spend your money for. Include the cost of **every** item you buy. Be specific, not general. For example, instead of using the general category of food, use more specific categories, such as groceries, lunch, snacks, and restaurants.

Try not to overlook anything you spend money on – even interest payments and investments. Keep your information in one place. At the end of each month, the number of items you have recorded will be quite large. Of course, the items will be disorganized, unrelated and difficult to understand. To make the information meaningful, consolidate the amounts of similar items, then organize them in major categories for your review.

Take adequate time to examine your list. Keep in mind that this is a list of **how much you spent** and **what you spent money for** during the past month. After you have thoroughly studied the list, ask yourself these questions:

- **Am I getting my money's worth?**
- **Am I satisfied with the way I am spending my money?**

It is extremely important that you take the time necessary to answer these questions. The answers will definitely affect your life. If your answer to either question is "no," focus your attention on the problem categories. If you do not like where you are spending your money, why not change? You have the opportunity **now** to change your habits and control your use of money. Why not try to get your money's worth? Why not be **absolutely satisfied** with the way you are spending your money?

This should not be a one-time exercise. Rather, it is a process worth following every month. **Your goal is to try to continuously refine the way you spend money so that you are satisfied with how the money is spent** – getting your money's worth. The benefits you will receive from this exercise will be directly proportional to the amount of effort and determination you put into it.

The lasting razor blade

I would like to share with you some examples of how my wife and I changed our spending habits in our early years.

The Lasting Razor Blade

One day years ago, after reviewing our expenses for one month, I became dissatisfied with the amount of money I was spending for razor blades. I said to myself, "If I use a razor blade for more than one day, I can lower my costs significantly." I decided to *use one blade for several days and invest the savings. Today razor blades for my new razor cost about $5 for five blades. If I were still using one blade a day, my cost would be about $30 a month. Now I use one blade for four days and have reduced my costs to 25 cents a day, a savings of $22.50 a month or $270 a year. Some of my friends claim they can use one blade for two weeks and one of them even for four weeks. How fortunate, but then all beards are not created equal.*

The peanut butter sandwich

The Peanut Butter Sandwich

Years ago, I became aware of how much money I was spending for lunches. Added together, the amount was sizable. I was also aware that I had been eating too much and gradually gaining weight. And yet, I was not eating what I enjoy most for lunch – a peanut butter sandwich. I decided I would solve three problems at the same time. If I brown-bagged lunch each day, I could:

Eat what I wanted (a peanut butter sandwich),
Eat less and lose weight,
Invest the difference.

This I did – and still do. If buying lunch costs $5 a day, the amount for one week is $25 and, for one month over $100 or more than $1,200 a year. By comparison, my peanut butter sandwich costs only about 50 cents a day or $130 a year. The rest is saved.

Street Parking

Thirty-five years ago, after reviewing our expenses one month, my wife made a suggestion. "Jim, you're spending $25 a month to park your car in a garage at work. Why don't you park your car on the street and save an additional $25 a month?" I reluctantly agreed. I had to walk five blocks out of the way, but she had found another $300 a year to invest.

The Fur Coat

It seems as though you always want something you can't afford. As newlyweds, our entertainment was walking and window shopping. One winter day we walked by an exclusive fur store. We stopped and admired one of the beautiful fur coats. I asked Virginia if she wanted it. She said she really did, and then added, "but we can't afford it because it would reduce our investment savings." We continued on our walk.

A year or so later, after we had saved some money, we happened to walk by the same store again. We stopped to look at the beautiful coats. I asked if she wanted one of them. This time Virginia didn't answer me right away. Finally, she said, "No, I don't want one." I asked why. She said, "If I had one, I would lose the earnings on the money it would take to buy the coat. Also, I would have to pay for insurance and storage. No, I would rather have my money working for me." This small incident taught me an important principle:

The process of accumulating money places a different sense of worth on the value of your wants NOW and the value you place on the money you have saved. If LATER you can afford to buy what you desired earlier, you often find that its appeal is gone and you no longer have a desire for it.

Planning Ahead for Financial Windfalls

It's helpful to plan ahead of time what you intend to do with money that others might give you. Why not plan that any financial windfall you receive outside of your regular current income will be invested to further improve your financial future?

Sticking to Our Decision

As I have stated, my wife and I decided when we were first married that if we were ever given money, we would save and invest it. We agreed we would not spend it, no matter how great the temptation. We intended to live within our own earned income.

Thirteen years into our marriage, I was unlucky and had an accident. I was pounding a piece of steel with a hammer when a piece of metal broke off and flew into my eye. I should have been wearing protective goggles but I wasn't, and as a result I lost one of my eyes.

My accident insurance policy paid me $100,000, a large sum of money. There was no question about what we were going to do with the money. My wife and I had decided years earlier that we would invest any windfall money. At that time we had numerous wants, but our biggest want, by far, was financial independence. This is why I invested the money. That investment alone is now worth well over $1 million. Of course I'd trade it back in a second, if I could, to restore the sight in my eye.

◆ Trying Other Ways to Find Extra Money

If you get a raise:

Consider putting a third of it aside for your future financial independence, rather than using all of it to increase your present standard of living.

Reduce costs for services:

Become a handy person and take care of your own repairs – but use safety goggles and other safety measures.

Share tools and equipment with friends and neighbors.

"Barter" your services by exchanging your time and special talents or skills for services or products.

Reduce costs of purchases and save on energy:

Buy a **good used luxury car** and save on depreciation – it tends to retain its value.

Own one car and participate in ride-sharing.

Purchase high-quality second-hand furniture.

Make your own clothing.

Take advantage of advertised and quantity discounts; buy in bulk.

Save money by buying in bulk.

Plan your errands in advance to minimize driving around town. This also helps to conserve our natural resources.

Eat out less and enjoy your own cooking.

If all else fails, maybe get a second job.

You may think the process of reviewing how money is spent is boring...

Enjoying Our Money's Worth

You may think the process of reviewing how money is spent is a boring and unproductive exercise. However, my wife and I have found it to be a great help. Our marriage started off in 1954 with a five-year-old car, a one-bedroom apartment, $1,000, loads of love, and the determination that we were going to become financially independent. In the ensuing years we have lived within our means after "paying ourselves first." At the same time, I believe that we

*have done **everything,** and I mean **everything,** that we have **truly
wanted** to do. We have chosen what we absolutely wanted, and we
believe we have received our money's worth.*

The personal incidents that I have described in the preceding pages
reflect a way of life that is not unique. Most people who have the determination to achieve financial independence find ways to save and invest.

We are all different and have different backgrounds and experiences
from which we can generate new ways of finding money to save. **You can
always find extra money to set aside if you are determined to do so.**

The Role of Social Security

The Role of Social Security

You cannot rely solely on Social Security benefits.

As part of your financial future, you've no doubt thought about Social Security. How much money are you likely to receive?

Social Security is a package of protection – for retirement, for survivors and for disability. It is intended to protect you and your family while you work and after you retire. **It is a base you can build on in combination with other insurance and investments**. You cannot rely **solely** on Social Security benefits. If you do, you may be very disappointed in your later years.

Social Security Benefits Can Provide Monthly Income:

- ◆ To you and to eligible members of your family if an illness or injury keeps you from working for a long period of time.
- ◆ For your survivors if you should die.
- ◆ To you and certain members of your family when you retire.

You cannot rely solely on Social Security benefits. If you do, you may be very disappointed in your later years.

How It Works

The first time you came into contact with Social Security was probably when you applied for your Social Security number. This number is the key to the protection you earn during your working lifetime.

If you are an employee, your employer deducts your share of the Social Security tax from your wages. Your employer adds a matching amount and sends a report of your wages to the Social Security Administration. The report shows your name, Social Security number, and how much you have earned. If you are self-employed, you pay your own Social Security tax and make your own report. You do this when you file your Federal income tax return.

Your reported wages or self-employment income is entered on your Social Security record. This record is used to figure the amount of benefits payable to you and your family when you retire or become disabled, or to your family if you die.

It is a good idea to check your Social Security record periodically to make sure your earnings have been correctly reported. This is especially important if you change jobs often. You can find this information by writing to any Social Security office, by calling **1-800-772-1213,** or by visiting their web site at **www.ssa.gov.**

The amount of your monthly retirement or disability benefits is determined by a rather complicated computation. Generally speaking, the amount of your benefit depends upon your average earnings over a period of years prior to your retirement or disability.

Health Insurance Under Medicare

Nearly all people age 65 and over are eligible for health insurance under Medicare. This includes some people who do not have enough credit for work covered by Social Security to qualify for monthly cash benefits upon their retirement. There are two parts to Medicare: hospital insurance and, for those who choose, medical insurance.

If you are 65 or over and entitled to Social Security, you are automatically eligible for hospital insurance.

The medical insurance part of Medicare is voluntary. No one is covered automatically. You will receive this protection only if you sign up for it within a specified period. Generally speaking, medical insurance will pay 80% of the "reasonable charges" for certain physician's services after the first $50 in each calendar year.

In making your plans for financial independence, you must take into account that benefit levels may be cut for people who retire in the future; and, in some cases, payouts could be eliminated for upper-income retirees. Medical expenses are one more frightening topic to consider as life expectancies lengthen and medical costs continue to soar.

Post-Retirement Strategies

*The dollar will continue to lose value
whether you retire or not.*

When you stop working and your personal earnings cease, there are three fundamental financial challenges you must face. You must:

- **Increase Your Emergency Reserve**
- **Determine the Allocation of Your Assets**
- **Decide the Amount of Money You Want Each Month From Each Source**

◆ Increase Your Emergency Reserve

In Chapter 7, "Planning for Emergencies," I described the purpose of establishing an emergency reserve.

Before your personal earnings cease, you need to consider adjusting your emergency reserve to an amount equal to six months or more expected living costs. In addition, you must be prepared to provide for taxes and unforeseen expenses. In determining the reserve, you might deduct from it the expected amount that you will receive from such sources as Social Security, a pension plan and any insurance annuity.

Most people don't want to take chances with their assets as they near retirement.

As an alternative, it is wise to consider your long-term investment as part of your emergency reserve, which could be used as collateral for a short-term loan.

The dollar will
continue to
lose value...

◆ Determine the Allocation of Your Assets

Most people don't want to "take chances" with their assets as they near retirement. They tend to become more financially conservative. "Conventional wisdom" suggests that people approaching retirement should shift all or a high percentage of their accumulated assets into fixed income securities. The motivation here is for people to feel secure in the knowledge that their assets are "safe." But can you afford to do this? In other words, **are you sure you will be secure**? Should your main concern be for the **safety of the number of dollars** OR **the future value of those dollars?**

It is wise to plan for the likelihood that **the dollar will continue to lose value whether you retire or not**. It is my belief the dollar can lose one-half of its value every 10 years. If you agree with me, can you afford to be so conservative that you tie your money to the value of a dollar?

Extremely Important Information

It is extremely important that you understand the dramatic effect the long-term loss in value of a dollar has on a fixed income investment.

The following two examples assume you invested $100,000 in a fixed income guaranteed investment on December 31, 1971, that paid an annual rate of return of 6%.

Example 1   *Fixed Amount for Entire Period*

You want to receive a $500 check each month for the first year.

The purpose of this example is to illustrate how the loss in value of a dollar adversely affects a fixed income investment over a long period of time.

Year End	Amount of Monthly Check	Total Amount Paid	Dollar Value Year End
1971			$100,000
1972	$500	$ 6,000	100,000
1973	500	12,000	100,000
1974	500	18,000	100,000
1975	500	24,000	100,000
1976	500	30,000	100,000
1977	500	36,000	100,000
1978	500	42,000	100,000
1979	500	48,000	100,000
1980	500	54,000	100,000
1981	500	60,000	100,000
1982	500	66,000	100,000
1983	500	72,000	100,000
1984	500	78,000	100,000
1985	500	84,000	100,000
1986	500	90,000	100,000
1987	500	96,000	100,000
1988	500	102,000	100,000
1989	500	108,000	100,000
1990	500	114,000	100,000
1991	500	120,000	100,000
1992	500	126,000	100,000
1993	500	132,000	100,000
1994	500	138,000	100,000
1995	500	144,000	100,000
1996	500	150,000	100,000
1997	500	156,000	100,000
1998	500	162,000	100,000

The last Dollar Value Year-end was $100,000 while the Total Amount Paid was $162,000.

From the end of 1971 to the end of 1998 the dollar **lost 77% of its value** at the average **rate of 2.85% a year**. Thus, the last $500 check would buy only what **$113** would buy in **1971.**

The year-end value of $100,000 would buy only what $23,000 would buy in 1971.

Can you afford to do this?

The dollar will continue to lose value whether you retire or not.

It is much better to learn how the shrinking value of a dollar can effect you over time, while there is still time for you to do something about it.

Can you afford to have more of your assets tied to the declining value of a dollar?

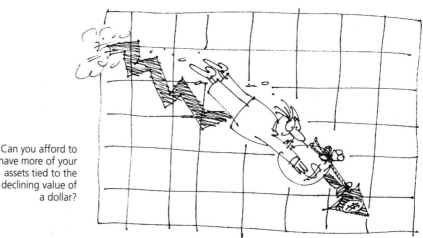

Example 2

Fixed Amount Each Month Increasing by 7.18% Each Year

You want to receive a $500 check each month for the first year. Thereafter, the amount of the check is increased by 7.18% each year. This rate will keep pace with the shrinking value of a dollar, assuming the dollar will lose one-half of its value every 10 years.

The purpose of this example is to illustrate how you can run out of money **trying to stay ahead of the shrinking value of a dollar** while investing in fixed income securities over the long term.

Year End	Amount of Monthly Check	Total Amount Paid	Dollar Value Year End
1971			$100,000
1972	$ 500	$ 6,000	100,000
1973	536	12,431	99,557
1974	574	19,323	98,612
1975	616	26,711	97,101
1976	660	34,629	94,950
1977	707	43,115	92,083
1978	758	52,211	88,412
1979	812	61,959	83,844
1980	871	72,408	78,275
1981	933	83,607	71,590
1982	1,000	95,610	63,667
1983	1,072	108,475	54,370
1984	1,149	122,263	43,549
1985	1,232	137,042	31,043
1986	1,320	152,881	16,675
1987	1,415	169,858	252

The last Dollar Value Year-end at 1987, 16 years from the initial investment, was only $252, while the Total Amount Paid was $169,858.

From the end of 1971 to the end of 1987 the dollar **lost 67% of its value** at the average **rate of 4.17% a year**. Thus, the last $1,415 check received would buy only what **$467** would buy in **1971**.

After 1987 there was no more money available to provide for additional monthly checks. Your resource had gone to zero.

As you can see, fixed income investments are unable to keep up with the continual loss in the value of a dollar over time.

What percentage of your assets should you keep in fixed income securities? The amount depends entirely on you. You must determine how much you can afford to have tied to the dollar over time. If you are attempting to keep a certain percent of your assets in fixed income securities, keep in mind that at retirement you already have a large amount of your assets in those securities – that is, if you are covered by Social Security, a pension plan or an insurance annuity. **Seldom do we think of placing value on the capital necessary to produce a monthly income for life, but this can be done quite simply.** For example, if your combined retirement income from such sources totals $1,200 a month, it would take $240,000 invested at 6% to produce that amount.

$1,200 a month x 12 months = $14,400 a year
this figure ÷ .06 (6%) = principal amount of $240,000.

Can you afford to have more of your assets tied to the declining value of a dollar?

The Consequences of Conservative Advice

People who suggest that you shift your assets to "safe" fixed income securities have probably not experienced the consequences of doing so. Take my case as an example. As I mentioned previously, in 1958 I traded $10,000 for shares of a common stock mutual fund, "Fund A." Those shares have grown in number by the reinvestment of all the distributions of dividends and capital gains over the years. I could trade these shares back for dollars to reinvest in fixed income securities, but would it be wise for me to do so?

If I did this I would be forced to realize an enormous taxable profit on the transaction. In fact, I would end up owing $205,477 in taxes. Obviously, this tax would reduce the amount I would have available to invest in fixed income funds.

(22-1)

Amount Lost in Shifting "Fund A" Shares to Dollars	
Amount received if traded "Fund A" back for dollars	$1,209,766
Less original cost	−10,000
Less reinvestments over the 36 years* from	
Dividends**..	− 39,952
Capital Gains..	− 572,738
Profit before taxes	$587,076
Taxes Due @ 35% Rate	**$205,477**

How Much Would be Available for Reinvestment?	
Amount received if traded "Fund A" back for dollars	$1,209,766
Less taxes due	−205,477
Less amount to pay off loan	−7,500
Amount available after taxes	$996,789
Percentage lost in this "shift"	**17.6%**

   * Taxes have already been paid.

  ** In Chapter 15, I discussed the desirability of investing in a mutual fund whose investment objective is growth in value rather than high dividend income. "Fund A" happens to be one of these funds. From this investment *all of the profits* came from growth except for the $39,952 which came from dividends. Do you see why I believe in investing in these types of mutual funds over time?

In this example, my $1,209,766 would immediately shrink by **18%** *to $996,789. If I took this amount and invested it in a money market fund, what would I receive? The typical average yield was 2.3% on December 31, 1993. This would give me $22,926 a year or $1,911 a month, provided the yield remained constant year after year. But this won't happen. The yield varies day to day, both up and down. For example, one year earlier in 1992 the yield was 3.04%.*

I would end up owing Uncle Sam $205,477 in taxes.

*The key point is that if I did this, I would be tying this investment to the value of a dollar. If a dollar loses half its value over the next 10 years, I may feel safe having the number of dollars, while I would actually be losing half the value of **my** dollars.*

I expect to live a normal length of life. During that time, I will need money to provide for what my wife and I want in the future. If, over the next 10 years, the value of a dollar falls to 50 cents, how will this affect my family? If I kept the money in a money market fund, I would still have the same $996,789 10 years from now. But, the value of those dollars will be worth only half as much, or $498,395. If the money market fund is still paying me $1,911 a month, I will still be receiving that many dollars, but the value of those dollars will be worth only $956. If I did this, I will have "carefully" lost a great deal of value over time. Where will I be able to find the extra dollars I will need to maintain my standard of living?

If I do not shift my assets to a fixed income fund, I will still have my shares of Fund A. Again, if the value of the dollar falls to 50 cents at the end of 10 years, where will I be? If Fund A will only keep pace with the loss in value of a dollar, the shares will be worth $2,419,532, not $1,209,766, because in 10 years the dollar would be worth only one-half as much as it was worth 10 years earlier. This is true only if Fund A keeps pace with the shrinking value of a dollar. Would it be wise for me to shift my assets into fixed income dollars? I think not, and I do not intend to do so.

◆ Decide the Amount You Want Each Month from Each Source

It is a common belief that income can be derived only from so-called **safe investments,** such as money market funds. You need to consider that there are other sources of money to provide for your future monthly wants.

They include:

Social Security

Insurance annuities

Interest from fixed income investments

Dividends from common stocks

Profits from the sale of common stocks

A fixed amount monthly from the sale of equity **mutual fund assets,** that is, a "Check-a-Month" plan.

Decide the source and amount of the money that you want each month.

Ideal Objectives for Monthly Payments When You Retire

If you believe as strongly as I do that a dollar will significantly lose value over time, what might the ideal objectives be for a personal strategy that will satisfy your desire to receive constant monthly payments from an investment?

You want the investment:

To be free from the shrinking value of a dollar.

To provide a known fixed amount on a certain day each month.

To be adjusted annually for the loss in value of a dollar.

Since there are so many potential sources of income, how do you know which one fits your desired objective best?

The following chart is designed to help you understand the possibilities.

(22-2)

How Do the Sources of Money Compare With the Ideal Monthly Payment Objectives?

Sources of Money	Ideal Monthly Payment Objectives		
	Free from Shrinking Value of a Dollar	Fixed Amount Certain Day Each Month	Adjusted Annually for Loss in Value of a Dollar*
Social Security and Pension Plans	No	Yes	No
Fixed Insurance Annuities	No	Yes	No
Interest from Fixed Income Investments	No	Yes	Unlikely
Dividends from Common Stocks	Yes	Maybe	Unlikely
Profits from the Sale of Common Stocks	Yes	Maybe	Maybe
A Fixed Monthly Amount from Sales of Equity Mutual Fund Assets (Check-A-Month Plan)	Yes	Yes	Yes

*The adjustment may not equal the actual loss in the value of a dollar.

When you compare the various sources of money described in the chart above, you may identify those that could produce the monthly payments that you want. Only one source (the Check-a-Month plan) definitely satisfies the three ideal monthly payment objectives. To accomplish your investment objectives, let's assume you have invested prior to your retirement in common stocks of a group of the most successful companies. Although most people have a tendency to be more conservative as they near retirement, I strongly believe **you should consider continuing the same investment strategy after retirement that you were following before.** Are you concerned that you will outlive your sources of income? Remember you may live another 20 to 30 years (or more!) and **the dollar will continue to lose value whether you retire or not.** Why not plan to have your investment last your lifetime and still have some remaining?

One of the sources of money in the preceding table describes how you can provide a fixed monthly amount from the sale of equity mutual fund assets.

The History of Check-a-Month

*When we first created American Century Mutual Funds in 1958, one of the funds paid quarterly dividends. The amount paid out each quarter varied according to the dividends the fund received from the portfolio investments during that quarter. These **amounts were unpredictable and erratic.** Moreover, any profits realized by the fund on portfolio sales during the year could only be paid in the final quarter of the year.*

*Fund investors complained bitterly because they wanted to know **what amount they would receive and when they would receive it.** Under the circumstances, it was impossible to meet their requests.*

*We began to realize many investors were dependent on their dividend checks as though they were paychecks. One possible solution to this problem was a simple, convenient and automatic plan that **assured investors they would receive a predetermined amount of money on a particular day of each month.***

Because of this, "Check-a-Month" was created. We decided to discontinue distributing quarterly dividends, and pay them only once a year. We offered instead a "Check-a-Month" while continuing to professionally manage the balance of the investors' shares.

Your check arrives by
the first of the month.
You can count on it.

A "Check-a-Month" Plan Example

The purpose of this example is to illustrate the impact of a Check-a-Month where the amount of the check is increased yearly to make sure your check amount is not eroded by the loss in value of a dollar. It is not the purpose to focus on investment results.

This plan is based on the historical performance of "Fund A," a fully-managed mutual fund that would produce a fixed monthly amount from the sale of mutual fund shares. **The example assumes that you traded $100,000 for shares of Fund A on December 31, 1971.** This amount was selected to make it easy for you to understand the results when used in multiples.

You initially instruct the fund that you want to receive a $500 check each month for the first year. Thereafter, in an attempt to compensate for the continued loss in value of a dollar, you instruct the fund to increase the Check-a-Month amount by 7.18% each year. This rate will keep pace with the shrinking dollar, assuming it will lose one-half of its value every 10 years.

The fund redeems enough shares on the 20th of each month to provide the amount you wanted, while the balance of your shares continues to be professionally managed. Your check arrives by the first of the month. You can count on it.

Any investment income and capital gain distributions have been reinvested in additional shares. Note – it is extremely important for you to be aware that **the fund in this example does not invest for dividend yield.** The fund's philosophy is that earnings, not dividends, are the main factor that drives the value of stocks. However, the fund will accept whatever dividends a company pays (the effect of any taxes **is not** considered).

The following table shows how the amount of your initial $500 monthly check increases each year in an effort to compensate for the loss in the value of a dollar.

(22-3)   *Check-A-Month Plan in "Fund A" For a Fixed Amount*
Part 1   *Each Month Increasing 7.18% Each Year*

Year End	Amount of Monthly Check	Accumulated Amount Redeemed	Value of Remaining Shares
1971			$ 100,000
1972	$500	$6,000	$137,603
1973	536	12,431	101,246
1974	574	19,323	64,068

But what happened to the value of your remaining shares at the end of each year? The value of your shares was affected by the collective attitudes of people in the marketplace, from extreme optimism to depression. Over the years these attitudes are affected by wars, recessions, inflation, peace, other major events, and optimism about the future. Keep in mind that when the market is at its lowest, you will be deluged by a constant stream of negative and discouraging news. Conversely, when the market is at its highest, you are overwhelmed by optimistic news, which gives you positive views about the future. In both instances, you must remain aware of what is happening and fight to prevent these emotional reactions from influencing your own rational judgment by focusing on your long-term financial goals.

Keep in mind that when the market is at its lowest, you will be deluged by a constant stream of negative and discouraging news.

The Value of Remaining Shares varied up and down from your initial $100,000 investment and by the end of 1974 amounted to only $64,068 (the stock market was absolutely battered in 1974). Since you did not have a crystal ball, you could not know which way the market might go. If you were not patient, if you were not optimistic about future opportunities, and if you did not remember that in the past the stock market,

over time, has always recovered any losses and continued to go to new highs, you probably would have become discouraged and terminated your investment plan. In doing so, you would have lost 35% on your investment in two years.

On the other hand, if you had remained patient, if you were optimistic about future opportunities, and if you had remembered that in the past the stock market, over time, had always recovered any losses and continued to new highs, you would probably have continued on with your plan.

In Table 22-3, note the end Value of Remaining Shares after 22 years was worth the amazing sum of $1,955,047, after you received a total of $300,610 in monthly payments.

From the end of 1971 to the end of 1993 the dollar lost 72% of its value at the average rate of 6% a year. Thus, the last check of $2,145 would buy only what $601 would buy in 1971.

The Value of Remaining Shares of $1,955,047 would buy only what $547,413 would buy in 1971, which is more than five times the original investment of $100,000.

This illustrates the importance of trying to stay ahead of inflation.

At this point I invite you to draw your own conclusions. Would these results be worth your patience and confidence? Do you think there would be any possibility of having similar results with a "safe" investment?

Keep in mind that this example was based on historical results of Fund A over a 22-year period from December 31, 1971, through December 1993. Of course, these results are not necessarily representative of all common stock mutual fund investments. What has happened in the past may be an indication of what could possibly occur again in the future, but it is highly unlikely that these results will happen in an identical fashion again. Future results will vary and may be better or worse than those of the past.

(22-3)   *Check-A-Month Plan in "Fund A" For a Fixed Amount*
Part 2   *Each Month Increasing 7.18% Each Year*

Year End	Amount of Monthly Check	Accumulated Amount Redeemed	Value of Remaining Shares
1971			$ 100,000
1972	$ 500	$ 6,000	$ 137,603
1973	536	12,431	101,246
1974	574	19,323	64,068
1975	616	26,711	83,163
1976	660	34,629	124,729
1977	707	43,115	132,447
1978	758	52,211	184,511
1979	812	61,959	307,726
1980	871	72,408	517,965
1981	933	83,607	477,753
1982	1,000	95,610	506,907
1983	1,072	108,475	617,798
1984	1,149	122,263	534,480
1985	1,232	137,042	698,735
1986	1,320	152,881	814,421
1987	1,415	169,858	906,792
1988	1,516	188,054	912,056
1989	1,625	207,556	1,283,433
1990	1,742	228,459	1,213,636
1991	1,867	250,862	2,021,990
1992	2,001	274,874	1,910,364
1993	2,145	300,610	1,955,047

If the amount of your Check-a-Month is too large, it is possible it will deplete your investment. Likewise, if the share value of your fund falls, your investment may be entirely depleted before the share price of your fund can rebound.

Investing requires patience . . .

. . . results don't spring up overnight.

I would like to be remembered for what I did for others rather than for what I did for myself.

JAMES E. STOWERS

I hope my messages have been clear. Obviously, I feel strongly about them. **It is my belief that once you're aware and fully understand what you can do, you don't have to be told by anyone what you should do. You will know what you want to do.**

We all have different wants and place different values on those wants. We also have varying degrees of determination to fulfill those wants. That is part of what makes each of us special.

Knowing what you want to do and doing it are two separate issues. Simply **wanting** is not enough. **I have learned over the years that determination and persistence make the difference.**

If you are absolutely determined to become financially independent, you can take the initiative and put these fundamental principles and ideas into use to help you reach your financial goals. To the wise investor, the world is a place full of opportunity where dreams can be realized.

Investing is like planting a tree. Like an acorn, even the smallest investment holds great potential, awaiting only time, nourishment, and the right place to grow.

Investing requires patience. Results don't spring up overnight. Those who look for growth too quickly may cause their sprouts to wither and die, while those who allow time for strong roots to form will almost certainly see their investments mature and flourish.

Because of market cycles, every long-term investment must pass through times that are less favorable to growth. But wise investors will keep their roots firmly planted, waiting patiently for the next growth cycle to come.

As your young investments grow, they can thrive on the attention provided by professional management, while regular investing keeps their growth steady.

When a well-tended investment grows to maturity, patient investors are rewarded, knowing that the strength and stability they sought were well worth the wait.

I recently read an article about finances that included this statement: **"Accumulating enough money is a goal for most of us, but for most it's not attainable."** I strongly disagree. True, most people **will not** accumulate enough money, but I absolutely disagree with the thought that most people **cannot** attain it.

I am convinced that everyone can become and remain financially independent, including you.

If You. . .

- ◆ **set your goal to do so,**
- ◆ **have enough time remaining,**
- ◆ **are aware of how much money it will take to provide what you want, whether you live or die,**
- ◆ **decide where you can go to invest your money to accomplish what you want,**
- ◆ **remain patient and give your investment time to grow,**
- ◆ **continue to remain absolutely determined,**

Then You Can . . .

achieve and remain financially independent.

In doing these things, however, chances are that you will have to re-examine and rearrange some of your priorities.

Sadly, it is true that most people will not attain financial independence because the temptation is far too great to spend and live well today rather than to invest in order to become financially independent tomorrow.

When people save, they are deferring gratification now, for a more rewarding experience in the future.

"The Best Is Yet To Be."

Important Note

This book includes the Stowers Financial Analysis CD especially designed to encourage you to think about your future financial health. If you are determined to improve your financial position, take time now to explore this interactive analysis and become aware of the ideas, principles, and facts that affect your personal future.

To gain additional financial insights, or to order this book and CD for family and friends, **call 1-800-234-3445,** or visit our website at **www.stowers-innovations.com.** We welcome your feedback.

The following tables further illustrate the power of compounding described in Chapter 4.

A1

How Much Cash Does It Take Monthly to Provide $100 a Month for 35 Years?
(From Age 65 to Age 100)

AGE AT START

(%)	20	30	40	50	60
0	$ 77.78	$100.00	$140.00	$233.33	$700.00
4	15.42	25.34	44.82	93.21	344.60
6	6.81	13.01	26.43	62.29	257.19
8	3.02	6.76	15.94	42.92	198.66
10	1.34	3.56	9.81	30.35	157.97
12	.60	1.89	6.13	21.93	128.69
14	.27	1.02	3.89	16.13	106.96
16	.13	.55	2.49	12.03	90.38
YEARS	45	35	25	15	5

PUT IN MONTHLY to age 65

A2

How Much Cash Does It Take Now to Provide $100 a Month for 35 Years?
(From Age 65 to Age 100)

AGE AT START

(%)	0	10	20	30	40	50	60
0	$42,000.00	$42,000.00	$42,000.00	$42,000.00	$42,000.00	$42,000.00	$42,000.00
4	1,781.84	2,637.55	3,904.22	5,779.20	8,554.63	12,662.95	18,744.25
6	404.83	724.99	1,298.35	2,325.15	4,163.99	7,457.07	13,354.48
8	97.40	210.28	453.98	980.10	2,115.97	4,568.22	9,862.44
10	24.66	63.97	165.92	430.36	1,116.25	2,895.28	7,509.60
12	6.54	20.30	63.05	195.82	608.18	1,888.93	5,866.71
14	1.80	6.69	24.79	91.90	340.70	1,263.05	4,682.41
16	.52	2.28	10.05	44.32	195.49	862.41	3,804.48
YEARS	65	55	45	35	25	15	5

PUT IN AT ONE TIME
to Age 65

A3   *Value of Investing $1.00 EACH MONTH at 10%**

Year	Amount Invested	Account Value	Year	Amount Invested	Account Value
1	12	$ 12.54	36	432	3,751.21
2	24	26.34	37	444	4,138.87
3	36	41.51	38	456	4,565.30
4	48	58.20	39	468	5,034.37
5	60	76.56	40	480	5,550.35
6	72	96.76	41	492	6,117.92
7	84	118.97	42	504	6,742.26
8	96	143.41	43	516	7,429.02
9	108	170.29	44	528	8,184.47
10	120	199.86	45	540	9,015.45
11	132	232.39	46	552	9,929.54
12	144	268.17	47	564	10,935.03
13	156	307.53	48	576	12,041.08
14	168	350.82	49	588	13,257.72
15	180	398.44	50	600	14,596.04
16	192	450.83	51	612	16,068.18
17	204	508.45	52	624	17,687.54
18	216	571.84	53	636	19,468.84
19	228	641.56	54	648	21,428.26
20	240	718.26	55	660	23,583.63
21	252	802.63	56	672	25,954.53
22	264	895.43	57	684	28,562.52
23	276	997.51	58	696	31,431.31
24	288	1,109.80	59	708	34,586.99
25	300	1,233.32	60	720	38,058.23
26	312	1,369.20	61	732	41,876.59
27	324	1,518.66	62	744	46,076.79
28	336	1,683.06	63	756	50,697.01
29	348	1,863.91	64	768	55,779.25
30	360	2,062.84	65	780	61,369.71
31	372	2,281.67			
32	384	2,522.38			
33	396	2,787.15			
34	408	3,078.41			
35	420	3,398.79			

A4   *Value of Investing $1.00 ONCE at 10%**

Year	Account Value	Year	Account Value
1	$1.10	36	30.91
2	1.21	37	34.00
3	1.33	38	37.40
4	1.46	39	41.14
5	1.61	40	45.26
6	1.77	41	49.79
7	1.95	42	54.76
8	2.14	43	60.24
9	2.36	44	66.26
10	2.59	45	72.89
11	2.85	46	80.18
12	3.14	47	88.20
13	3.45	48	97.02
14	3.80	49	106.72
15	4.18	50	117.39
16	4.59	51	129.13
17	5.05	52	142.04
18	5.56	53	156.25
19	6.12	54	171.87
20	6.73	55	189.06
21	7.40	56	207.97
22	8.14	57	228.76
23	8.95	58	251.64
24	9.85	59	276.80
25	10.83	60	304.48
26	11.92	61	334.93
27	13.11	62	368.42
28	14.42	63	405.27
29	15.86	64	445.79
30	17.45	65	490.37
31	19.19		
32	21.11		
33	23.23		
34	25.55		
35	28.10		

*Compounded Annually

B1

Amount of Investment......... $10,000 One Time
Investment in......... "Fund A"
(With All Distributions Reinvested)
Time Period Covered......... 7-1-1971 through 3-31-1994
(Progressing one quarter at a time)

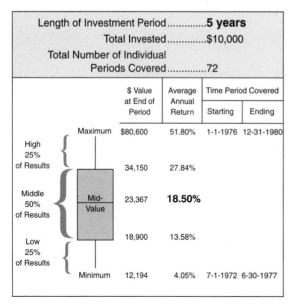

Length of Investment Period.............1 year
Total Invested.............$10,000
Total Number of Individual
Periods Covered.............88

		$ Value at End of Period	Annual Return	Time Period Covered Starting	Ending
	Maximum	$19,055	90.55%	4-1-1980	3-31-1981
High 25% of Results		14,541	45.41%		
Middle 50% of Results	Mid-Value	12,293	**22.93%**		
Low 25% of Results		9,846	-1.54%		
	Minimum	5,175	-48.25%	10-1-1973	9-30-1974

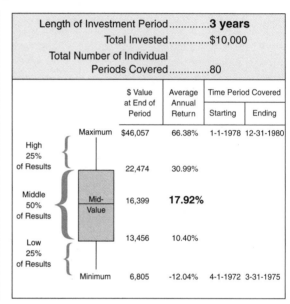

Length of Investment Period.............3 years
Total Invested.............$10,000
Total Number of Individual
Periods Covered.............80

		$ Value at End of Period	Average Annual Return	Time Period Covered Starting	Ending
	Maximum	$46,057	66.38%	1-1-1978	12-31-1980
High 25% of Results		22,474	30.99%		
Middle 50% of Results	Mid-Value	16,399	**17.92%**		
Low 25% of Results		13,456	10.40%		
	Minimum	6,805	-12.04%	4-1-1972	3-31-1975

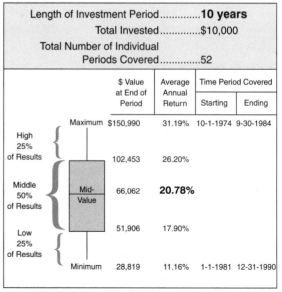

Length of Investment Period.............5 years
Total Invested.............$10,000
Total Number of Individual
Periods Covered.............72

		$ Value at End of Period	Average Annual Return	Time Period Covered Starting	Ending
	Maximum	$80,600	51.80%	1-1-1976	12-31-1980
High 25% of Results		34,150	27.84%		
Middle 50% of Results	Mid-Value	23,367	**18.50%**		
Low 25% of Results		18,900	13.58%		
	Minimum	12,194	4.05%	7-1-1972	6-30-1977

Length of Investment Period.............10 years
Total Invested.............$10,000
Total Number of Individual
Periods Covered.............52

		$ Value at End of Period	Average Annual Return	Time Period Covered Starting	Ending
	Maximum	$150,990	31.19%	10-1-1974	9-30-1984
High 25% of Results		102,453	26.20%		
Middle 50% of Results	Mid-Value	66,062	**20.78%**		
Low 25% of Results		51,906	17.90%		
	Minimum	28,819	11.16%	1-1-1981	12-31-1990

Not Drawn to Scale.

B2

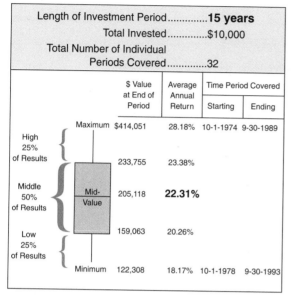

Length of Investment Period.............**15 years**
Total Invested.............$10,000
Total Number of Individual
Periods Covered.............32

	$ Value at End of Period	Average Annual Return	Time Period Covered	
			Starting	Ending
Maximum	$414,051	28.18%	10-1-1974	9-30-1989
High 25% of Results	233,755	23.38%		
Middle 50% of Results (Mid-Value)	205,118	**22.31%**		
Low 25% of Results	159,063	20.26%		
Minimum	122,308	18.17%	10-1-1978	9-30-1993

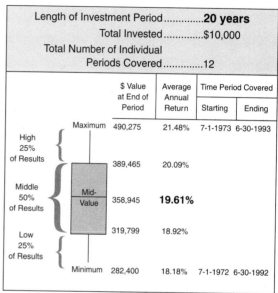

Length of Investment Period.............**20 years**
Total Invested.............$10,000
Total Number of Individual
Periods Covered.............12

	$ Value at End of Period	Average Annual Return	Time Period Covered	
			Starting	Ending
Maximum	490,275	21.48%	7-1-1973	6-30-1993
High 25% of Results	389,465	20.09%		
Middle 50% of Results (Mid-Value)	358,945	**19.61%**		
Low 25% of Results	319,799	18.92%		
Minimum	282,400	18.18%	7-1-1972	6-30-1992

Not Drawn to Scale.

B3 (17-1)   *$10,000 Investments in "Fund A"*

(With All Dividends Reinvested)

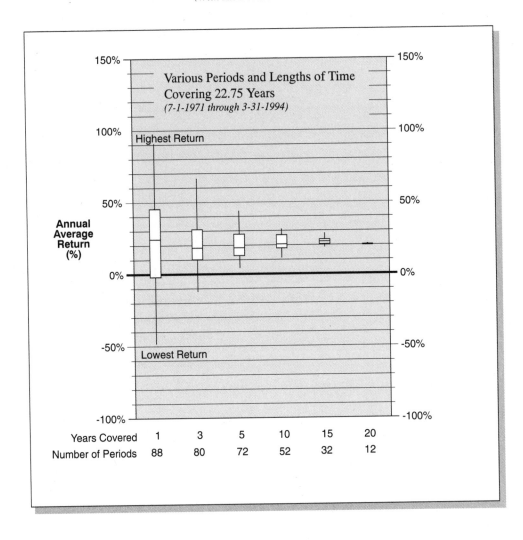

B 4

Amount of Investment......... $10,000 One Time
Investment in......... Dow Jones Industrial Average
(With All Distributions Reinvested)
Time Period Covered......... 7-1-1971 through 3-31-1994
(Progressing one quarter at a time)

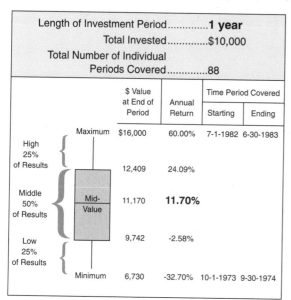

Length of Investment Period..............**1 year**
Total Invested..............$10,000
Total Number of Individual
Periods Covered..............88

		$ Value at End of Period	Annual Return	Time Period Covered Starting	Ending
	Maximum	$16,000	60.00%	7-1-1982	6-30-1983
High 25% of Results		12,409	24.09%		
Middle 50% of Results	Mid-Value	11,170	**11.70%**		
Low 25% of Results		9,742	-2.58%		
	Minimum	6,730	-32.70%	10-1-1973	9-30-1974

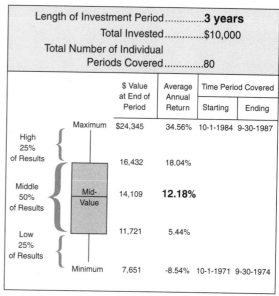

Length of Investment Period..............**3 years**
Total Invested..............$10,000
Total Number of Individual
Periods Covered..............80

		$ Value at End of Period	Average Annual Return	Time Period Covered Starting	Ending
	Maximum	$24,345	34.56%	10-1-1984	9-30-1987
High 25% of Results		16,432	18.04%		
Middle 50% of Results	Mid-Value	14,109	**12.18%**		
Low 25% of Results		11,721	5.44%		
	Minimum	7,651	-8.54%	10-1-1971	9-30-1974

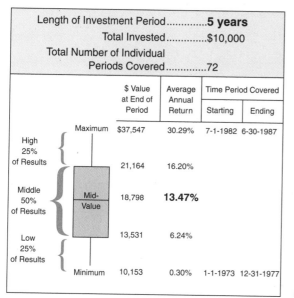

Length of Investment Period..............**5 years**
Total Invested..............$10,000
Total Number of Individual
Periods Covered..............72

		$ Value at End of Period	Average Annual Return	Time Period Covered Starting	Ending
	Maximum	$37,547	30.29%	7-1-1982	6-30-1987
High 25% of Results		21,164	16.20%		
Middle 50% of Results	Mid-Value	18,798	**13.47%**		
Low 25% of Results		13,531	6.24%		
	Minimum	10,153	0.30%	1-1-1973	12-31-1977

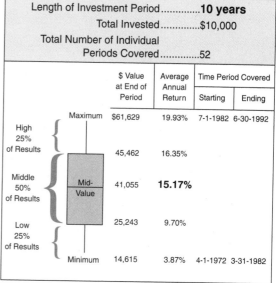

Length of Investment Period..............**10 years**
Total Invested..............$10,000
Total Number of Individual
Periods Covered..............52

		$ Value at End of Period	Average Annual Return	Time Period Covered Starting	Ending
	Maximum	$61,629	19.93%	7-1-1982	6-30-1992
High 25% of Results		45,462	16.35%		
Middle 50% of Results	Mid-Value	41,055	**15.17%**		
Low 25% of Results		25,243	9.70%		
	Minimum	14,615	3.87%	4-1-1972	3-31-1982

Not Drawn to Scale.

B5

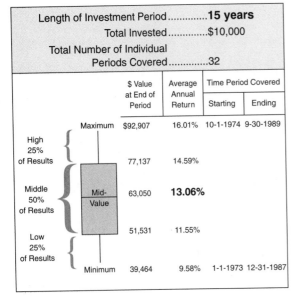

		$ Value at End of Period	Average Annual Return	Time Period Covered Starting	Time Period Covered Ending
	Maximum	$92,907	16.01%	10-1-1974	9-30-1989
High 25% of Results		77,137	14.59%		
Middle 50% of Results	Mid-Value	63,050	**13.06%**		
		51,531	11.55%		
Low 25% of Results					
	Minimum	39,464	9.58%	1-1-1973	12-31-1987

Length of Investment Period..............**15 years**
Total Invested..............$10,000
Total Number of Individual Periods Covered..............32

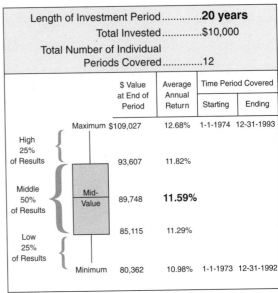

		$ Value at End of Period	Average Annual Return	Time Period Covered Starting	Time Period Covered Ending
	Maximum	$109,027	12.68%	1-1-1974	12-31-1993
High 25% of Results		93,607	11.82%		
Middle 50% of Results	Mid-Value	89,748	**11.59%**		
		85,115	11.29%		
Low 25% of Results					
	Minimum	80,362	10.98%	1-1-1973	12-31-1992

Length of Investment Period..............**20 years**
Total Invested..............$10,000
Total Number of Individual Periods Covered..............12

Not Drawn to Scale.

B6

$10,000 Investments in Dow Jones Industrial Average
(With All Dividends Reinvested)

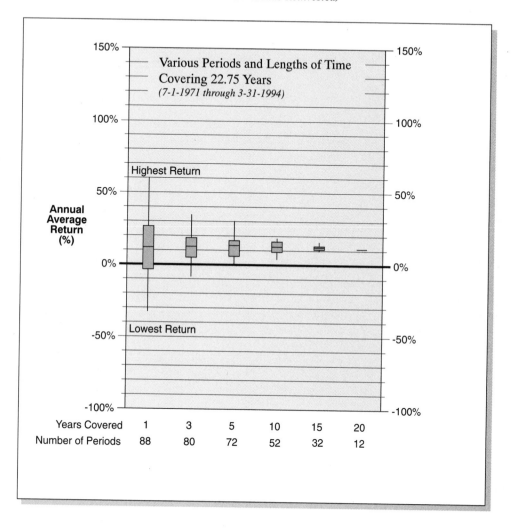

B7

Amount of Investment......... $10,000 One Time
Investment in......... Standard & Poor's 500
(*With All Distributions Reinvested*)
Time Period Covered......... 7-1-1971 through 3-31-1994
(*Progressing one quarter at a time*)

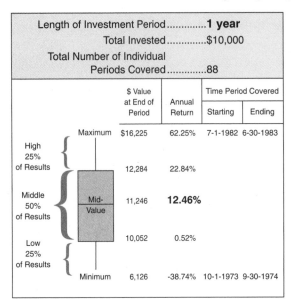

Length of Investment Period..............**1 year**				
Total Invested..............$10,000				
Total Number of Individual Periods Covered..............88				

	$ Value at End of Period	Annual Return	Time Period Covered	
			Starting	Ending
Maximum	$16,225	62.25%	7-1-1982	6-30-1983
High 25% of Results	12,284	22.84%		
Middle 50% of Results (Mid-Value)	11,246	**12.46%**		
Low 25% of Results	10,052	0.52%		
Minimum	6,126	-38.74%	10-1-1973	9-30-1974

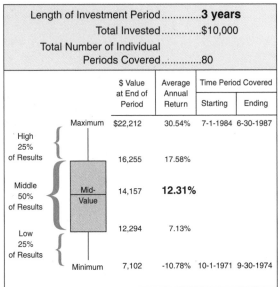

Length of Investment Period..............**3 years**				
Total Invested..............$10,000				
Total Number of Individual Periods Covered..............80				

	$ Value at End of Period	Average Annual Return	Time Period Covered	
			Starting	Ending
Maximum	$22,212	30.54%	7-1-1984	6-30-1987
High 25% of Results	16,255	17.58%		
Middle 50% of Results (Mid-Value)	14,157	**12.31%**		
Low 25% of Results	12,294	7.13%		
Minimum	7,102	-10.78%	10-1-1971	9-30-1974

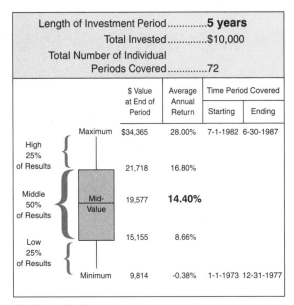

Length of Investment Period..............**5 years**				
Total Invested..............$10,000				
Total Number of Individual Periods Covered..............72				

	$ Value at End of Period	Average Annual Return	Time Period Covered	
			Starting	Ending
Maximum	$34,365	28.00%	7-1-1982	6-30-1987
High 25% of Results	21,718	16.80%		
Middle 50% of Results (Mid-Value)	19,577	**14.40%**		
Low 25% of Results	15,155	8.66%		
Minimum	9,814	-0.38%	1-1-1973	12-31-1977

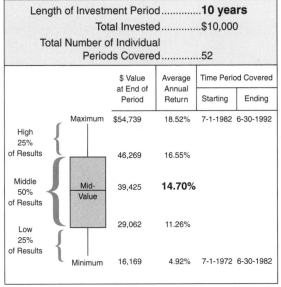

Length of Investment Period..............**10 years**				
Total Invested..............$10,000				
Total Number of Individual Periods Covered..............52				

	$ Value at End of Period	Average Annual Return	Time Period Covered	
			Starting	Ending
Maximum	$54,739	18.52%	7-1-1982	6-30-1992
High 25% of Results	46,269	16.55%		
Middle 50% of Results (Mid-Value)	39,425	**14.70%**		
Low 25% of Results	29,062	11.26%		
Minimum	16,169	4.92%	7-1-1972	6-30-1982

Not Drawn to Scale.

B8

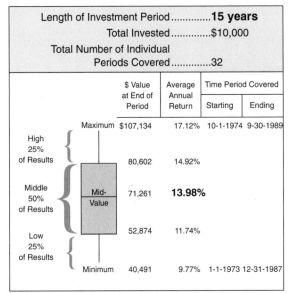

	$ Value at End of Period	Average Annual Return	Time Period Covered	
			Starting	Ending
Maximum	$107,134	17.12%	10-1-1974	9-30-1989
High 25% of Results	80,602	14.92%		
Middle 50% of Results	71,261	**13.98%**		
Low 25% of Results	52,874	11.74%		
Minimum	40,491	9.77%	1-1-1973	12-31-1987

Length of Investment Period.............**15 years**
Total Invested.............$10,000
Total Number of Individual Periods Covered.............32

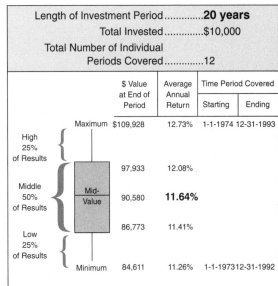

	$ Value at End of Period	Average Annual Return	Time Period Covered	
			Starting	Ending
Maximum	$109,928	12.73%	1-1-1974	12-31-1993
High 25% of Results	97,933	12.08%		
Middle 50% of Results	90,580	**11.64%**		
Low 25% of Results	86,773	11.41%		
Minimum	84,611	11.26%	1-1-1973	12-31-1992

Length of Investment Period.............**20 years**
Total Invested.............$10,000
Total Number of Individual Periods Covered.............12

Not Drawn to Scale.

B9   *$10,000 Investments in Standard & Poor's 500*

(With All Dividends Reinvested)

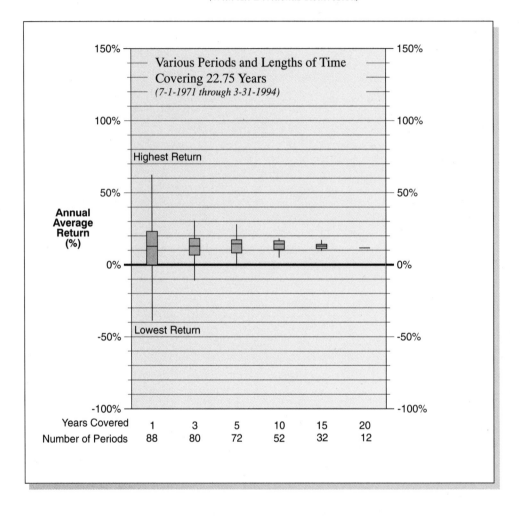

B10

One-Year Results
$10,000 One-Time Investments
(With All Dividends Reinvested)

Results of "Fund A" Compared with
the Results of Dow Jones Industrial Average *and* Standard & Poor's 500

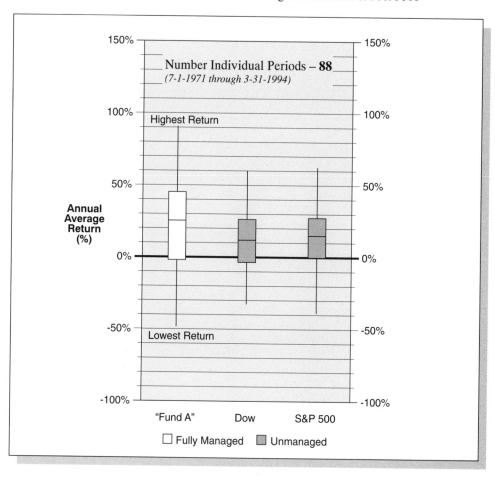

B11

Three-Year Results
$10,000 One-Time Investments
(*With All Dividends Reinvested*)

Results of "Fund A" Compared with
the Results of Dow Jones Industrial Average *and* Standard & Poor's 500

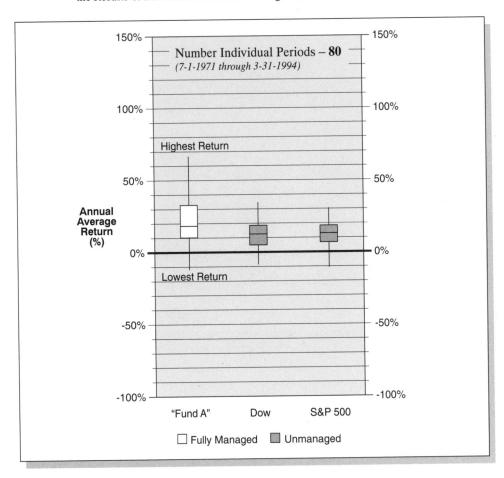

B12

Five-Year Results
$10,000 One-Time Investments
(With All Dividends Reinvested)

Results of "Fund A" Compared with
the Results of Dow Jones Industrial Average *and* Standard & Poor's 500

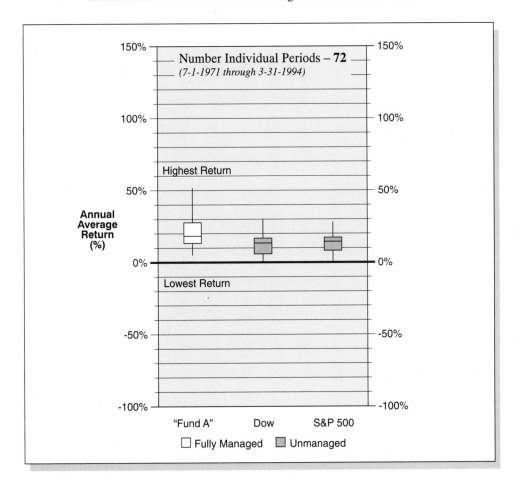

B13

10-Year Results
$10,000 One-Time Investments
(With All Dividends Reinvested)

Results of "Fund A" Compared with
the Results of Dow Jones Industrial Average *and* Standard & Poor's 500

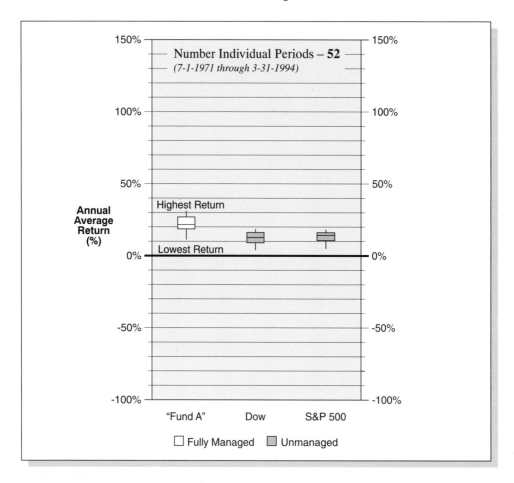

B14

15-Year Results
$10,000 One-Time Investments
(With All Dividends Reinvested)

Results of "Fund A" Compared with
the Results of Dow Jones Industrial Average *and* Standard & Poor's 500

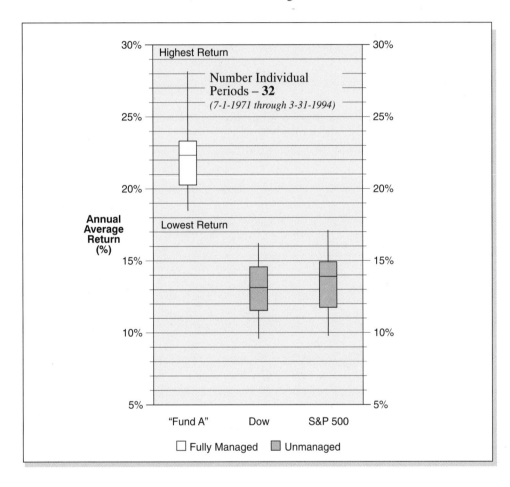

B15 (17-3)

20-Year Results
$10,000 One-Time Investments
(With All Dividends Reinvested)

Results of "Fund A" Compared with
the Results of Dow Jones Industrial Average *and* Standard & Poor's 500

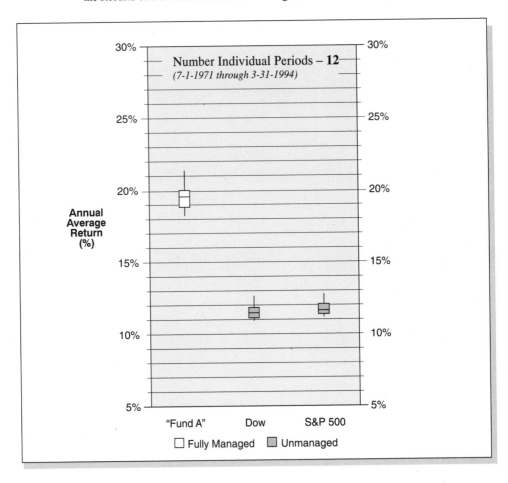

B16 (17-4A)   *The Probabilities of Receiving a Certain Return*
$10,000 One-Time Investment
(With All Dividends Reinvested)

Comparing "Fund A" results with those of Dow Jones Industrial Average and Standard & Poor's 500

Covering 22.75 Years (7-1-1971 through 3-31-1994)
*Percentage Results **in Excess of** Various Compound Rates*

PERIOD (YEARS) — "Fund A" — **NUMBER OF PERIODS**

PERIOD (YEARS)	0%	2%	4%	6%	8%	10%	12%	14%	16%	18%	20%	22%	24%	26%	28%	30%	NUMBER OF PERIODS
1	72	72	67	65	64	61	60	57	57	54	53	51	50	46	42	39	88
3	91	90	87	87	83	77	71	67	60	50	46	41	35	31	30	27	80
5	100	100	100	97	94	88	81	72	62	54	44	37	33	31	25	23	72
10	100	100	100	100	100	100	98	88	82	75	57	46	42	28	15	3	52
15	100	100	100	100	100	100	100	100	100	100	78	59	18	6	3	0	32
20	100	100	100	100	100	100	100	100	(100)	33	0	0	0	0	0		12

PERIOD (YEARS) — **Dow Jones Industrial Average** — **NUMBER OF PERIODS**

PERIOD (YEARS)	0%	2%	4%	6%	8%	10%	12%	14%	16%	18%	20%	22%	24%	26%	28%	30%	NUMBER OF PERIODS
1	72	71	67	64	60	53	48	44	39	37	32	28	27	22	20	19	88
3	91	85	81	75	70	61	51	45	36	26	17	6	5	3	3	3	80
5	100	97	84	77	69	65	59	48	27	19	15	8	4	4	4	1	72
10	100	100	96	86	84	75	65	55	32	13	0	0	0	0	0	0	52
15	100	100	100	100	100	93	71	34	3	0	0	0	0	0	0	0	32
20	100	100	100	100	100	(100)	25	0	0	0	0	0	0	0	0	0	12

PERIOD (YEARS) — **Standard & Poor's 500** — **NUMBER OF PERIODS**

PERIOD (YEARS)	0%	2%	4%	6%	8%	10%	12%	14%	16%	18%	20%	22%	24%	26%	28%	30%	NUMBER OF PERIODS
1	77	71	70	69	62	60	54	48	42	38	30	26	25	22	21	18	88
3	91	88	87	81	73	62	53	46	38	23	12	6	5	5	2	1	80
5	98	95	90	84	79	70	63	56	27	13	8	4	4	4	1	0	72
10	100	100	100	94	86	82	75	61	34	3	0	0	0	0	0	0	52
15	100	100	100	100	100	96	75	50	9	0	0	0	0	0	0	0	32
20	100	100	100	100	100	(100)	33	0	0	0	0	0	0	0	0	0	12

(100) Represents the highest rate of return occurring for **all** the 20-year investment periods.

C1

Amount of Investment......... $100 a Month
Investment in......... "Fund A"
(With All Distributions Reinvested)
Time Period Covered......... 7-1-1971 through 3-31-1994
(Progressing one quarter at a time)

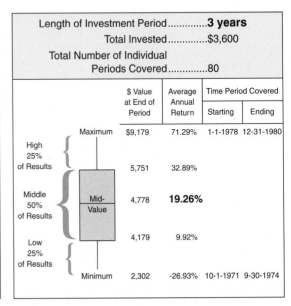

Length of Investment Period.............1 year
Total Invested.............$1,200
Total Number of Individual Periods Covered.............88

		$ Value at End of Period	Annual Return	Time Period Covered	
				Starting	Ending
Maximum		$1,932	128.70%	10-1-1977	9-30-1978
High 25% of Results		1,563	60.16%		
Middle 50% of Results	Mid-Value	1,446	**39.89%**		
Low 25% of Results		1,273	11.42%		
Minimum		899	-42.69%	10-1-1973	9-30-1974

Length of Investment Period.............3 years
Total Invested.............$3,600
Total Number of Individual Periods Covered.............80

		$ Value at End of Period	Average Annual Return	Time Period Covered	
				Starting	Ending
Maximum		$9,179	71.29%	1-1-1978	12-31-1980
High 25% of Results		5,751	32.89%		
Middle 50% of Results	Mid-Value	4,778	**19.26%**		
Low 25% of Results		4,179	9.92%		
Minimum		2,302	-26.93%	10-1-1971	9-30-1974

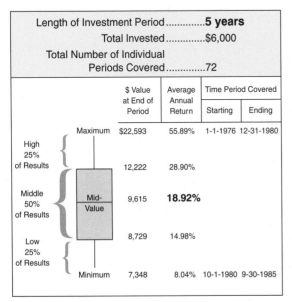

Length of Investment Period.............5 years
Total Invested.............$6,000
Total Number of Individual Periods Covered.............72

		$ Value at End of Period	Average Annual Return	Time Period Covered	
				Starting	Ending
Maximum		$22,593	55.89%	1-1-1976	12-31-1980
High 25% of Results		12,222	28.90%		
Middle 50% of Results	Mid-Value	9,615	**18.92%**		
Low 25% of Results		8,729	14.98%		
Minimum		7,348	8.04%	10-1-1980	9-30-1985

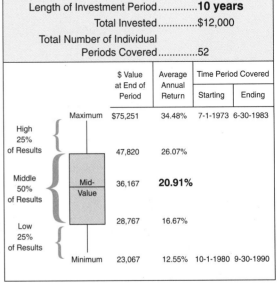

Length of Investment Period.............10 years
Total Invested.............$12,000
Total Number of Individual Periods Covered.............52

		$ Value at End of Period	Average Annual Return	Time Period Covered	
				Starting	Ending
Maximum		$75,251	34.48%	7-1-1973	6-30-1983
High 25% of Results		47,820	26.07%		
Middle 50% of Results	Mid-Value	36,167	**20.91%**		
Low 25% of Results		28,767	16.67%		
Minimum		23,067	12.55%	10-1-1980	9-30-1990

Not Drawn to Scale.

C2

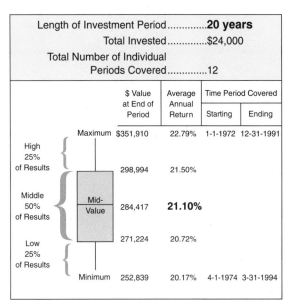

		$ Value at End of Period	Average Annual Return	Time Period Covered	
				Starting	Ending
	Maximum	$179,577	27.11%	10-1-1972	9-30-1987
High 25% of Results		126,042	23.13%		
Middle 50% of Results	Mid-Value	112,021	**21.80%**		
		88,638	19.15%		
Low 25% of Results					
	Minimum	63,830	15.40%	4-1-1979	3-31-1994

Length of Investment Period..............**15 years**
Total Invested..............$18,000
Total Number of Individual Periods Covered..............32

		$ Value at End of Period	Average Annual Return	Time Period Covered	
				Starting	Ending
	Maximum	$351,910	22.79%	1-1-1972	12-31-1991
High 25% of Results		298,994	21.50%		
Middle 50% of Results	Mid-Value	284,417	**21.10%**		
		271,224	20.72%		
Low 25% of Results					
	Minimum	252,839	20.17%	4-1-1974	3-31-1994

Length of Investment Period..............**20 years**
Total Invested..............$24,000
Total Number of Individual Periods Covered..............12

Not Drawn to Scale.

C3 (17-5) *$100-a-Month Investments in "Fund A"*

(With All Dividends Reinvested)

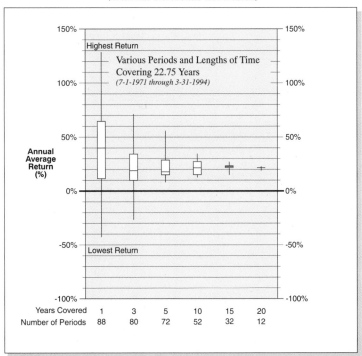

Various Periods and Lengths of Time Covering 22.75 Years
(7-1-1971 through 3-31-1994)

Years Covered	1	3	5	10	15	20
Number of Periods	88	80	72	52	32	12

C4

Amount of Investment......... $100 a Month
Investment in......... Dow Jones Industrial Average
(With All Distributions Reinvested)
Time Period Covered......... 7-1-1971 through 3-31-1994
(Progressing one quarter at a time)

Length of Investment Period..............**1 year**
Total Invested..............$1,200
Total Number of Individual Periods Covered..............88

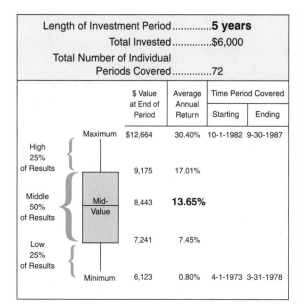

	$ Value at End of Period	Annual Return	Time Period Covered Starting	Ending
Maximum	$1,608	68.16%	4-1-1985	3-30-1986
High 25% of Results	1,335	21.40%		
Middle 50% of Results (Mid-Value)	1,282	**14.45%**		
Low 25% of Results	1,208	1.23%		
Minimum	911	-41.14%	10-1-1973	9-30-1974

Length of Investment Period..............**3 years**
Total Invested..............$3,600
Total Number of Individual Periods Covered..............80

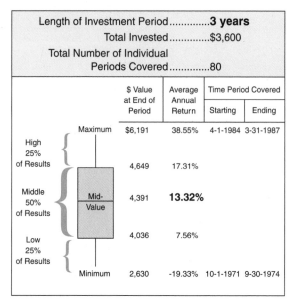

	$ Value at End of Period	Average Annual Return	Time Period Covered Starting	Ending
Maximum	$6,191	38.55%	4-1-1984	3-31-1987
High 25% of Results	4,649	17.31%		
Middle 50% of Results (Mid-Value)	4,391	**13.32%**		
Low 25% of Results	4,036	7.56%		
Minimum	2,630	-19.33%	10-1-1971	9-30-1974

Length of Investment Period..............**5 years**
Total Invested..............$6,000
Total Number of Individual Periods Covered..............72

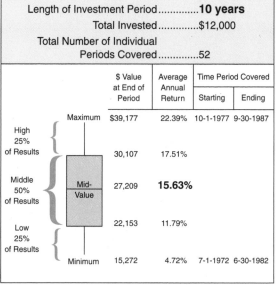

	$ Value at End of Period	Average Annual Return	Time Period Covered Starting	Ending
Maximum	$12,664	30.40%	10-1-1982	9-30-1987
High 25% of Results	9,175	17.01%		
Middle 50% of Results (Mid-Value)	8,443	**13.65%**		
Low 25% of Results	7,241	7.45%		
Minimum	6,123	0.80%	4-1-1973	3-31-1978

Length of Investment Period..............**10 years**
Total Invested..............$12,000
Total Number of Individual Periods Covered..............52

	$ Value at End of Period	Average Annual Return	Time Period Covered Starting	Ending
Maximum	$39,177	22.39%	10-1-1977	9-30-1987
High 25% of Results	30,107	17.51%		
Middle 50% of Results (Mid-Value)	27,209	**15.63%**		
Low 25% of Results	22,153	11.79%		
Minimum	15,272	4.72%	7-1-1972	6-30-1982

Not Drawn to Scale.

C5

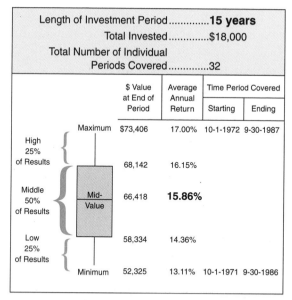

		$ Value at End of Period	Average Annual Return	Time Period Covered	
				Starting	Ending
	Maximum	$73,406	17.00%	10-1-1972	9-30-1987
High 25% of Results		68,142	16.15%		
Middle 50% of Results	Mid-Value	66,418	**15.86%**		
		58,334	14.36%		
Low 25% of Results					
	Minimum	52,325	13.11%	10-1-1971	9-30-1986

Length of Investment Period.............**15 years**
Total Invested.............$18,000
Total Number of Individual Periods Covered.............32

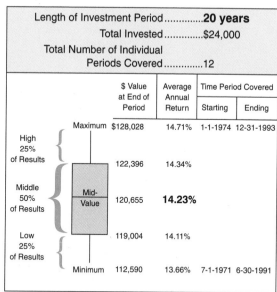

		$ Value at End of Period	Average Annual Return	Time Period Covered	
				Starting	Ending
	Maximum	$128,028	14.71%	1-1-1974	12-31-1993
High 25% of Results		122,396	14.34%		
Middle 50% of Results	Mid-Value	120,655	**14.23%**		
		119,004	14.11%		
Low 25% of Results					
	Minimum	112,590	13.66%	7-1-1971	6-30-1991

Length of Investment Period.............**20 years**
Total Invested.............$24,000
Total Number of Individual Periods Covered.............12

Not Drawn to Scale.

C6   *$100-a-Month Investments in Dow Jones Industrial Average*

(With All Dividends Reinvested)

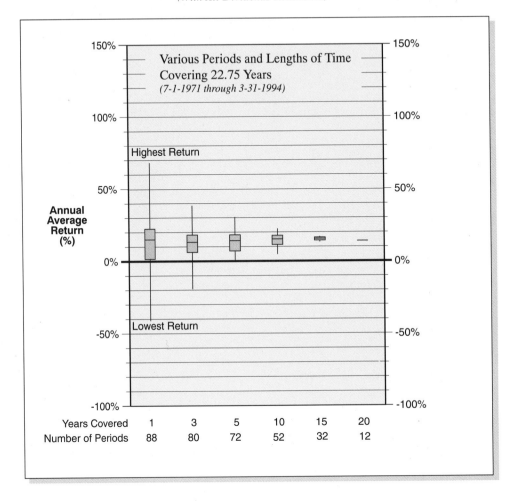

C7

Amount of Investment......... $100 a Month
Investment in......... Standard & Poor's 500
(With All Distributions Reinvested)
Time Period Covered......... 7-1-1971 through 3-31-1994
(Progressing one quarter at a time)

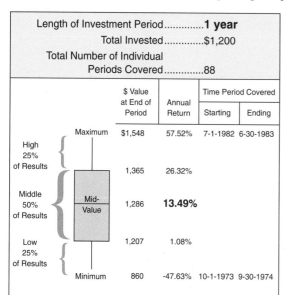

| Length of Investment Period.............**1 year** |
| Total Invested.............$1,200 |
| Total Number of Individual Periods Covered.............88 |

	$ Value at End of Period	Annual Return	Time Period Covered	
			Starting	Ending
Maximum	$1,548	57.52%	7-1-1982	6-30-1983
High 25% of Results	1,365	26.32%		
Middle 50% of Results (Mid-Value)	1,286	**13.49%**		
Low 25% of Results	1,207	1.08%		
Minimum	860	-47.63%	10-1-1973	9-30-1974

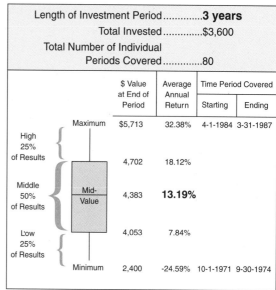

| Length of Investment Period.............**3 years** |
| Total Invested.............$3,600 |
| Total Number of Individual Periods Covered.............80 |

	$ Value at End of Period	Average Annual Return	Time Period Covered	
			Starting	Ending
Maximum	$5,713	32.38%	4-1-1984	3-31-1987
High 25% of Results	4,702	18.12%		
Middle 50% of Results (Mid-Value)	4,383	**13.19%**		
Low 25% of Results	4,053	7.84%		
Minimum	2,400	-24.59%	10-1-1971	9-30-1974

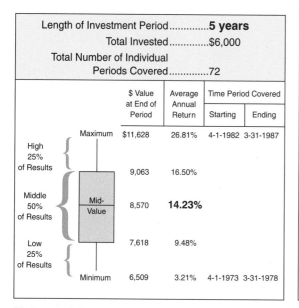

| Length of Investment Period.............**5 years** |
| Total Invested.............$6,000 |
| Total Number of Individual Periods Covered.............72 |

	$ Value at End of Period	Average Annual Return	Time Period Covered	
			Starting	Ending
Maximum	$11,628	26.81%	4-1-1982	3-31-1987
High 25% of Results	9,063	16.50%		
Middle 50% of Results (Mid-Value)	8,570	**14.23%**		
Low 25% of Results	7,618	9.48%		
Minimum	6,509	3.21%	4-1-1973	3-31-1978

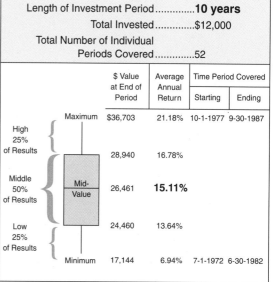

| Length of Investment Period.............**10 years** |
| Total Invested.............$12,000 |
| Total Number of Individual Periods Covered.............52 |

	$ Value at End of Period	Average Annual Return	Time Period Covered	
			Starting	Ending
Maximum	$36,703	21.18%	10-1-1977	9-30-1987
High 25% of Results	28,940	16.78%		
Middle 50% of Results (Mid-Value)	26,461	**15.11%**		
Low 25% of Results	24,460	13.64%		
Minimum	17,144	6.94%	7-1-1972	6-30-1982

Not Drawn to Scale.

C8

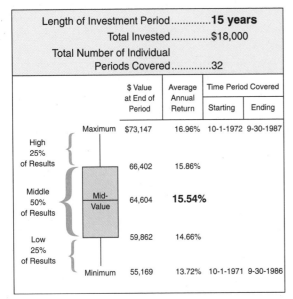

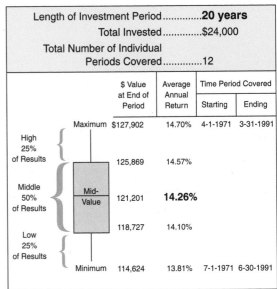

Not Drawn to Scale.

C9   *$100-a-Month Investments in Standard & Poor's 500*

(With All Dividends Reinvested)

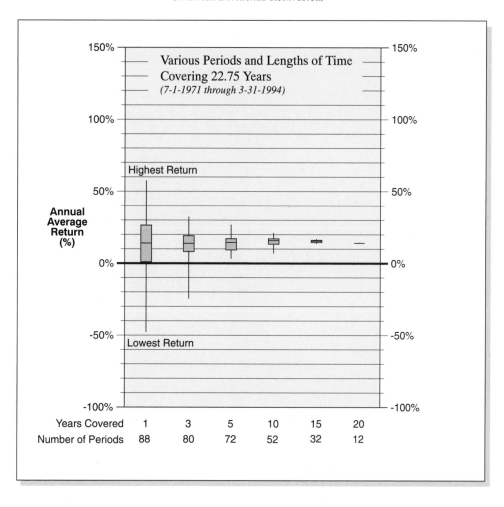

C10

One-Year Results
$100 a Month
(With All Dividends Reinvested)

Results of "Fund A" Compared with
the Results of Dow Jones Industrial Average *and* Standard & Poor's 500

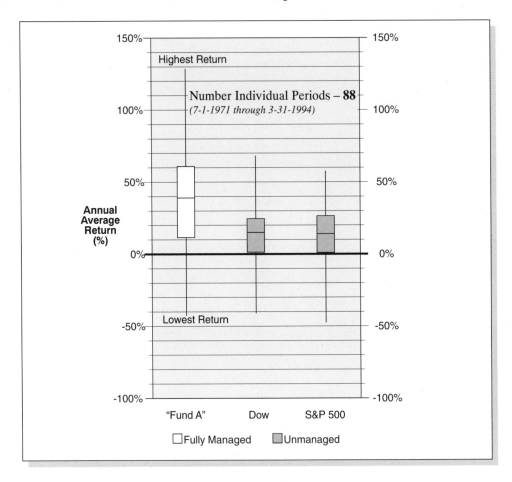

C11

Three-Year Results
$100 a Month
(With All Dividends Reinvested)

Results of "Fund A" Compared with
the Results of Dow Jones Industrial Average *and* Standard & Poor's 500

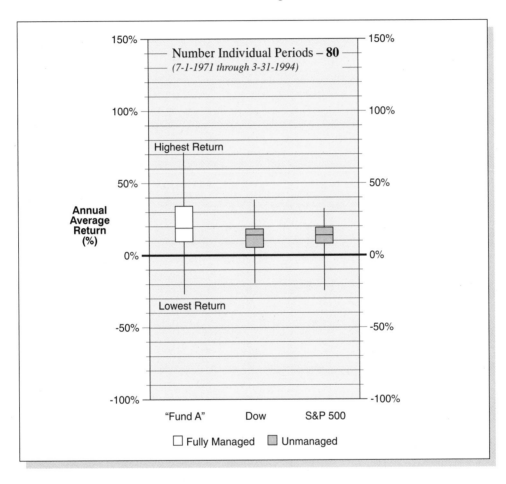

C12

Five-Year Results
$100 a Month
(With All Dividends Reinvested)

Results of "Fund A" Compared with
the Results of Dow Jones Industrial Average *and* Standard & Poor's 500

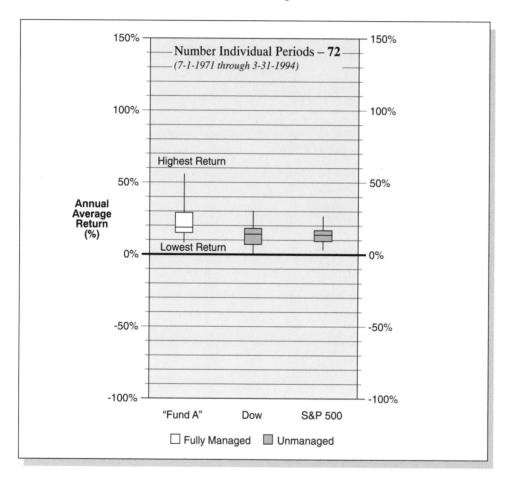

C13

10-Year Results
$100 a Month
(With All Dividends Reinvested)

Results of "Fund A" Compared with
the Results of Dow Jones Industrial Average *and* Standard & Poor's 500

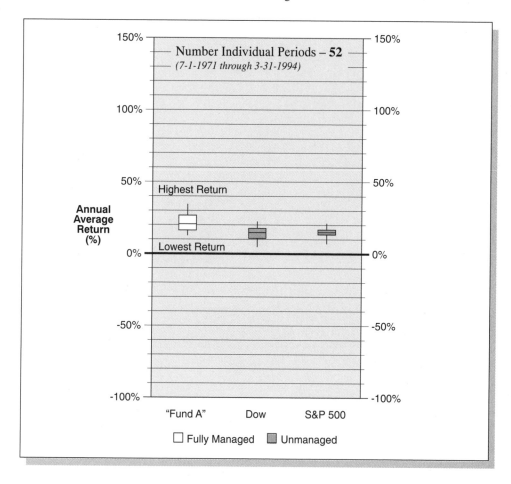

C14

15-Year Results
$100 a Month
(With All Dividends Reinvested)

Results of "Fund A" Compared with
the Results of Dow Jones Industrial Average *and* Standard & Poor's 500

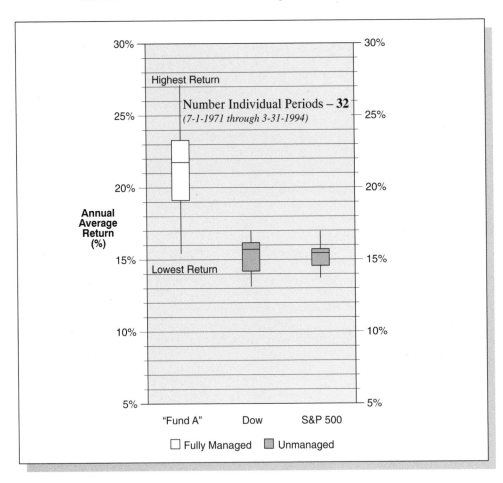

C15 (17-7)

20-Year Results
$100 a Month
(With All Dividends Reinvested)

Results of "Fund A" Compared with
the Results of Dow Jones Industrial Average *and* Standard & Poor's 500

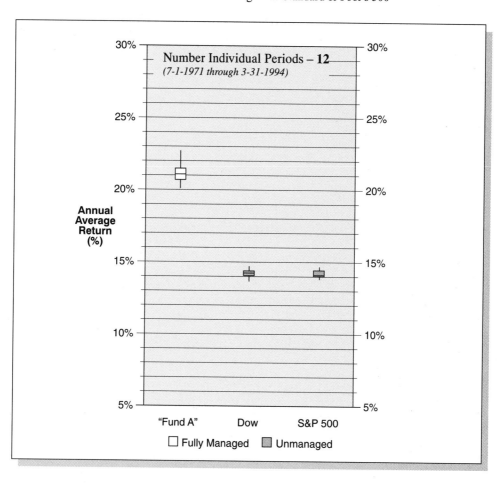

C16 (17-8A)

The Probabilities of Receiving a Certain Return

$100 A MONTH Investments

(With All Dividends Reinvested)

Comparing "Fund A" results with those of Dow Jones Industrial Average *and* Standard & Poor's 500

Covering 22.75 Years (7-1-1971 through 3-31-1994)
*Percentage Results in **Excess of** Various Compound Rates*

"Fund A"

PERIOD (YEARS)	0%	2%	4%	6%	8%	10%	12%	14%	16%	18%	20%	22%	24%	26%	28%	30%	NUMBER OF PERIODS
1	84	84	82	80	80	78	75	73	71	69	64	62	60	59	57	55	88
3	95	95	92	90	86	75	70	66	62	53	48	47	45	40	35	35	80
5	100	100	100	100	100	94	86	81	68	59	47	43	36	31	27	23	72
10	100	100	100	100	100	100	100	96	78	57	51	50	44	26	17	13	52
15	100	100	100	100	100	100	100	100	96	84	65	50	15	6	0	0	32
20	100	100	100	100	100	100	100	100	100	100	(100)	8	0	0	0	0	12

Dow Jones Industrial Average

PERIOD (YEARS)	0%	2%	4%	6%	8%	10%	12%	14%	16%	18%	20%	22%	24%	26%	28%	30%	NUMBER OF PERIODS
1	76	73	71	67	64	61	55	51	43	39	31	23	22	21	17	13	88
3	92	86	82	77	72	66	56	43	32	22	15	13	10	7	6	6	80
5	100	98	95	86	75	70	59	47	33	22	12	9	6	6	4	2	72
10	100	100	100	92	88	86	75	65	48	17	5	1	0	0	0	0	52
15	100	100	100	100	100	100	100	87	37	0	0	0	0	0	0	0	32
20	100	100	100	100	100	100	(100)	83	0	0	0	0	0	0	0	0	12

Standard & Poor's 500

PERIOD (YEARS)	0%	2%	4%	6%	8%	10%	12%	14%	16%	18%	20%	22%	24%	26%	28%	30%	NUMBER OF PERIODS
1	78	73	71	70	69	59	55	45	42	36	34	29	27	26	20	18	88
3	92	90	87	80	76	64	56	49	40	26	22	12	9	7	5	4	80
5	100	100	98	94	84	73	65	51	26	16	12	6	6	4	0	0	72
10	100	100	100	100	94	90	86	71	40	13	5	0	0	0	0	0	52
15	100	100	100	100	100	100	100	93	21	0	0	0	0	0	0	0	32
20	100	100	100	100	100	100	(100)	91	0	0	0	0	0	0	0	0	12

(100) Represents the highest rate of return occurring for **all** the 20-year investment periods.

Index of Charts and Graphs

ADDENDUM CHARTS

Annual Compound Rate – The annual rate at which money would have to increase or compound to reach the cumulative figure resulting from annual total returns. It is a discount rate and different from average annual return.

Annual Rate of Return – Annual percentage return after taxes that actually occurs or is anticipated on an investment. In common stock, the rate of return equals its dividend yield – calculated by dividing the annual dividend by the original purchase price. Rate of return may also refer to the total return, which is capital appreciation plus the dividend. In fixed income securities such as bonds and preferred stock, the rate of return equals the current yield, which is the coupon or dividend rate divided by the original purchase price.

Appreciation – An increase in value.

Assets – An item of value that is owned by a business, institution or individual.

Bonds – An interest bearing document used as a means for the government or business to raise money. The issuer (borrower) promises to pay the bondholder (creditor) a specified amount of interest for a specified time period and to repay the debt at maturity. Obligations that are due in more than one year are classified as bonds whereas if the debt is for less than one year, it is called a "note." Bondholders are creditors of the issuer and they do not have ownership privileges.

Capital Assets – Regarding individuals, any kind of investment. In relation to corporations, besides security investments, it includes fixed assets such as land, buildings, equipment and furniture. Generally, a capital asset can be any item that is not bought or sold in the normal course of business.

Capital Gains – The positive difference between an asset's purchase price and the selling price. Current tax regulations require any gains to be taxed at a rate up to 28%.

Certificates of Deposit – A money market instrument issued by banks that has a set interest rate and maturity date. CDs may be issued for as low as $100. CDs that are in denominations of $100,000 or more are called "jumbo CDs." Maturities can range from a few weeks to several years.

Closed-End Investment Company – Term used interchangeably with "closed-end fund." It is an investment company that issues a fixed number of shares and is listed on a major stock exchange. An investor who wishes to buy shares must purchase them from an investor who wishes to sell their shares. They do not deal with the investment company directly. In addition, an investor who wishes to sell their shares of a closed-end fund, must find a buyer.

Collateral – Assets, such as securities, that are pledged to a lender by a borrower. The assets secure the loan until the borrower repays it. In the event the borrower is unable to pay, the lender has the legal right to sell the assets to pay off the loan.

Common Stocks – Securities which represent an ownership interest in a public corporation. Owners are entitled to vote on the selection of directors and other important matters as well as to receive dividends when they are declared. If a corporation is liquidated, the claims of secured and unsecured creditors, bondholders and owners of preferred stock have priority over the claims of common stockholders.

Compounding – Increasing or combining; adding something that increases.

Corporate Bonds – Debt instrument issued by a corporation. In contrast to most municipal and government bonds, which are not traded on major exchanges and are tax-free, corporate bonds are traded on major exchanges and the interest paid to the investor is taxable.

Deductibles – Expenses that can be subtracted from an individual's adjusted gross income to obtain their taxable income. The type of expense deductions allowed is determined by the Internal Revenue Service (IRS). Examples include state and local taxes, charitable contributions and mortgage interest paid.

Distributions – 1: The payment, to investors, of realized capital gains on securities within the portfolio of a mutual fund or closed-end investment company. 2: Sale of a large block of securities over a period to avoid a decline in their prices. Technical analysts consider distribution patterns to predict when the security's price will fall.

Diversified Investment Company – Term used for either closed or open-ended mutual funds or unit trusts that invest in many different kinds of securities and companies. Under the Investment Company Act of 1940, an investment company, with respect to 75% of its portfolio, may not have more than 5% of its assets invested in the securities of any one issuer and may not own more than 10% of the voting shares of any one issuer.

Dividend – Distribution of a company's earnings to its shareholders, usually in the form of a quarterly check. The company's board of directors authorize and determine the amount of the dividend. Dividends are taxed as income in the year they are received by the shareholder. A mutual fund dividend is paid out of income and the shareholder's tax is dependent on whether the distributions originated from interest income, capital gains, or dividends received by the fund.

Dividend Reinvestment Plan – A program in which a dividend paying company (especially mutual funds) will automatically reinvest an investor's dividend to purchase additional shares of the company's stock. The dividend is still taxable by the IRS. In participating in this type of program, investors use dollar cost averaging to increase their amount of capital in the stock.

Dow Jones Industrial Average – Average of the prices of 30 well-known, predominantly blue-chip, industrial stocks. It is the oldest and most widely quoted of the marketing indicators.

Earned Income – Income generated from employment, pensions or annuities – for example, wages, salary, commissions, bonuses, IRAs, etc.

Earnings – The amount of profit a corporation receives after expenses and taxes are paid.

Equity Funds – Mutual funds that invest in common stocks (or ownership interests in public corporations).

Exchange Value – The amount that could be received in a trade or exchange.

Exemptions – IRS-allowed direct reductions from gross income. Personal and dependency exemptions are allowed for: individual taxpayers; elderly and disabled taxpayers; dependent children and other dependents more than half of whose support is provided; total or partial blindness; and a taxpayer's spouse.

Fixed Income – A security that pays a fixed rate of return, such as a bond or preferred stock. Fixed income investments offer protection against market risk, but do not protect holders against the risk of inflation.

Fully-Managed Fund – A mutual fund which allows the investment managers broad authority to use their best judgment to determine what to invest in, where to invest, how much to invest, how long to invest and how much cash to hold if attractive investments cannot be found. Minimal limitations are placed on the management of the fund.

Government Bonds – US government debt obligations that the government has promised to repay.

Gross Income – Total personal income before exclusions and deductions.

Income – Money, or other benefit, received from working, investments, etc.

Inflation – The persistent and appreciable rise in the prices of goods and services. Moderate inflation is normally associated with periods of expansion and high employment – increasing dollars chasing a dwindling supply of goods. Hyperinflation, when prices rise 100% or more a year, causes people to lose confidence in the currency. During inflationary times, people often divert their investments into real estate and gold because they usually retain their value.

Inflation Hedge – Investment designed to protect against the loss of purchasing power from inflation.

Insurance Annuity Income – The income or money received as a result of a contract between a life insurance company and an individual. This contract guarantees income for a defined period, usually starting at retirement, to the person on whose life the contract is based. In exchange, the individual agrees to make periodic payment to the insurance company. All capital in the annuity grows tax-deferred.

Interest – Dollar cost that a borrower pays a lender for the use of the lender's money.

Interest Rates – Rate of interest charged for the use of money, usually expressed at an annual rate. The rate is figured by dividing the amount of interest by the amount of principal borrowed.

Intrinsic Value – Genuine or real value.

Investment Objective – Financial objective that an investor or fund manager uses to determine which kind of investment is appropriate.

Leveraging – Method of enhancing return or value without increasing investment. For instance, leveraging is using borrowed money to own an investment that is expected to provide higher earnings and profits than the cost of borrowing.

Liability – The claims by creditors against a corporation or an individual. A corporation's liabilities include accounts payable, wages payable, dividends declared payable, accrued taxes payable, and long-term liabilities (bank loans and debentures).

Liquidity – The ability to buy or sell an asset quickly and in large volume without substantially affecting the asset's price. Liquidity also refers to the ability to convert to cash quickly.

Load Funds – Mutual funds that charge a fee when investors make purchases. This fee (or "load" as it is called) is used primarily to compensate salespeople selling the fund.

Maturity – The date on which the principal amount of a loan, bond, or any other debt instrument becomes due and is to be paid in full.

Municipal Bonds – A debt obligation issued by a state, state agency or authority, or a political subdivision, such as county, city, town or village. They may be issued for general governmental needs or special projects. Issuance must be approved by referendum or by an electoral body.

Before the Tax Reform Act of 1986, interest paid on municipal bonds was exempt from federal income tax and state and local income tax within the issuing state. The terms municipal and tax-exempt were synonymous. However, the Act separated municipal bonds into two broad groups – public purpose bonds and private purpose bonds. Public purpose bonds are tax-exempt and may be issued without limitations. Private purpose bonds are taxable unless specifically exempted. The difference between public and private purpose bonds is based on the percentage in which the bonds benefit private parties.

Mutual Fund – An open-end investment that offers the investor the benefits of portfolio diversification (provides greater safety and reduced volatility), and professional management. The shares are redeemable on demand at their net asset value. The fund invests the pooled assets into various investment vehicles including stocks, bonds, options, commodities and money market securities. How the fund invests is determined by the fund's objectives. The mutual fund's prospectus details this type of information plus information on any fees, the management company and other relevant data.

Net Asset Value (NAV) – An open-ended mutual fund's per share market value. In mutual funds, the net asset value is synonymous with "bid price" and "redemption price". In no-load funds, the NAV is also the asked price. They are all one figure. In load funds, the asked price is quoted after the sales charge is added to the net asset value. Most funds compute the NAV after the close of the exchanges each day. It is calculated by taking the closing market value of all securities within the fund plus all other assets (i.e., cash), subtracting all liabilities, then dividing the result (total net assets) by the total number of outstanding shares. The total number of outstanding shares usually varies daily because of redemptions and purchases.

No-Load Funds – A mutual fund that allows shares to be purchased without a sales charge imposed on its investors.

Non-Diversified Investment Company – A company that is not diversified. See definition of Diversified Investment Company.

Open-End Investment Company – A management investment company that issues new shares on demand when people buy them. The shares are bought at net asset value and may be redeemed back to the management company at any time at the current market price. Commonly called a "mutual fund," the type of vehicle that the shareholder's funds are invested in is dependent on the type of fund and its objectives.

Portfolio – The holdings of more than one stock, bond, cash equivalent or other asset by an individual or institution. A portfolio may be designed to achieve the investors goals – such as obtaining maximum returns or reducing risk through diversification.

Premium – Fee paid to an insurance company for insurance protection. Also, the single or multiple payments made to build an annuity fund.

Principal – 1: The face value or par value of a debt instrument that is separate from interest. 2: A person's capital, or the amount invested. 3: An employee of a securities firm who has supervisory responsibilities.

Probate – Process whereby a decedent's will is presented to a court and an executor is appointed to handle the settlement of the will.

Profits – The difference between a security's purchase price and selling price. If the selling price is higher than the purchase price, there is a profit. Conversely, if the selling price is lower than the purchase price, there is a loss.

Prospectus – A printed document that summarizes a corporation's registration statement for a new issue of non-exempt securities that was filed with the SEC. It details material information about the corporation and the security being issued. A prospectus must be given to all buyers and potential buyers of the new issue.

A preliminary prospectus is given to investors when brokers obtain indications of interest. Although the document does not have all the information included in the offering circular, it does include the major facts. A preliminary prospectus is often called a "red herring" because its front-page notice is printed in red ink. The notice states that the preliminary prospectus is "subject to completion or amendment" and "shall not constitute an offer to sell...".

Rates of Return – 1: In common stock, the rate of return equals its dividend yield – calculated by dividing the annual dividend by the original purchase price. Rate of return may also refer to the total return, which is capital appreciation plus the dividend. 2: In fixed-income securities such as bonds and preferred stock, the rate of return equals the current yield, which is the coupon or dividend rate divided by the original purchase price.

Securities – Any instrument that represents ownership, or the right to ownership, of a corporation, or that represents the debt of a corporation.

Self-Insured – When the assets accumulated are equal or greater than the amount of money needed for future security.

Share – A single unit of ownership in a corporation or mutual fund.

Standard & Poor's 500 Index (S&P 500) – A composite index that tracks 500 industrial, transportation, public utility, and financial stocks. The selection of stocks included in the index is determined by Standard & Poor's Corporation, which also publishes the index.

Stock Market – An organized marketplace where members gather to trade securities. Members may act either as agents for customers, or as principals for their own accounts.

Stock Market Indicator – Measurement utilized by technical analysts to make forecasts regarding the direction of the overall market or the movement of a particular stock.

Transfer of Ownership – 1: Process whereby a seller's broker delivers the certificates to the buyer's broker to effect a legal change of ownership. 2: To record the change of ownership on a corporation's books by its transfer agent. The buyer's name is recorded and all dividends, financial reports, proxies, and other literature are mailed directly to the new owner.

Trust Instrument – A legal document that establishes a fiduciary relationship in which a person, called a trustee, controls the spending of assets for the benefit of another person, called a beneficiary.

12b-1 Charges – A fee charged by some mutual funds to help cover the fund's sales and marketing expenses. The 12b-1 fee typically ranges from .25% of net assets in the case of some no-load funds that use it to cover advertising and marketing costs, to as high as 8.5%, the maximum allowed under National Association of Securities Dealers (NASD) rules. The primary use of 12b-1 fees is in funds sold through brokers, insurance agents, and financial planners.

Yield – An investment's return from dividends or interest expressed as a percentage of either cost at purchase or the investment's current price. For example, a security with a current market value of $36 a share paying a dividend of $2.50 annually will give an investor a return of 7% ($2.50/$36.00).

James E. Stowers
Author

James E. Stowers is founder and chairman of the board of the American Century Companies, a family of mutual funds located in Kansas City, Missouri. Stowers started the funds in 1958 with just $107,000 in assets from 24 shareholders. Today, the company manages over $100 billion in assets and serves more than two million shareholders.

Stowers holds two degrees from the University of Missouri. He was an Air Force fighter pilot during World War II, and remains an avid pilot. He and his wife, Virginia, live in Kansas City, Missouri.

The Stowers have recently begun one of the most important projects of their lives: creating the Stowers Institute for Medical Research, aspiring to be one of the world's premier biomedical research facilities, with the goal of freeing humanity from the dread of cancer and other gene-based diseases.
You can learn about the Stowers Institute at www.stowers-institute.org.

Jack Jonathan
President, Stowers Innovations, Inc.

Jack Jonathan's interest in book publishing and graphic arts began in the early 1940s while he was working with the United States Office of War Information and the United States Information Agency in Cairo, Egypt. Some of his most creative and productive years in publishing were spent working with Joyce Hall, founder of Hallmark Cards, in the early 1950s. After his retirement from Hallmark, Jonathan continued to apply his extensive knowledge of publishing and product development for the Swarovski Group in Europe. Currently, as president of Stowers Innovations, Jonathan continues to create and publish innovative extensions of Jim Stowers' philosophies to help people improve their financial positions.

Paul Coker Jr.
Illustrator

Paul Coker Jr. is a freelance cartoonist from Lawrence, Kansas. His drawings appear regularly in *MAD Magazine* and on Hallmark greeting cards. He has also developed characters for Rankin/Bass television productions, including "Frosty the Snowman." Coker hopes reading this book will make him financially independent. Meanwhile, he keeps working.

Rick Cusick
Book Designer

Rick Cusick is a well-known book designer and calligrapher whose work has appeared in numerous exhibitions and publications both in the United States and abroad. He formerly taught Typography and Editorial & Publication Design at the University of Kansas. Cusick is currently at work assembling an exhibition focusing on his work in the book arts. His 1987 one-man exhibition of lettering and typography appeared at the Appleman Gallery in London.

Rey Iway
Systems Analyst & Application Developer

Rey Iway is an independent computer consultant who has been designing and developing computer applications since 1974. His experience has given him the opportunity to do extensive work with financial and manufacturing systems and database design. Iway converted, redesigned and reprogrammed Mr. Stowers original mainframe application to run on the PC.